Values of Growth

Values of Growth

Critical Choices
for Americans

Volume VI

Lexington Books
D.C. Heath and Company
Lexington, Massachusetts
Toronto   London

Library of Congress Cataloging in Publication Data

Main entry under title:

Values of growth.

   (Critical choices for Americans; v. 6)
   Prepared under the auspices of the Commission on Critical Choices for
Americans.
   Includes index.
   1. Environmental policy—Addresses, essays, lectures. 2. Food supply—
Addresses, essays, lectures. 3. Population—Addresses, essays, lectures.
4. Agriculture and state—United States—Addresses, essays, lectures.
I. Commission on Critical Choices for Americans. II. Series.

HC79.E5V26   301.31   75-44724
ISBN 0-669-00418-9

Published simultaneously in Canada.

Printed in the United States of America.

International Standard Book Number: 0-669-00418-9

Library of Congress Catalog Card Number: 75-44724

Foreword

The Commission on Critical Choices for Americans, a nationally representative, bipartisan group of forty-two prominent Americans, was brought together on a voluntary basis by Nelson A. Rockefeller. After assuming the Vice Presidency of the United States, Mr. Rockefeller, the chairman of the Commission, became an ex officio member. The Commission's assignment was to develop information and insights which would bring about a better understanding of the problems confronting America. The Commission sought to identify the critical choices that must be made if these problems are to be met.

The Commission on Critical Choices grew out of a New York State study of the Role of a Modern State in a Changing World. This was initiated by Mr. Rockefeller, who was then Governor of New York, to review the major changes taking place in federal-state relationships. It became evident, however, that the problems confronting New York State went beyond state boundaries and had national and international implications.

In bringing the Commission on Critical Choices together, Mr. Rockefeller said:

As we approach the 200th Anniversary of the founding of our Nation, it has become clear that institutions and values which have accounted for our astounding progress during the past two centuries are straining to cope with the massive problems of the current era. The increase in the tempo of change and the vastness and complexity of the wholly new situations which are evolving with accelerated change, create a widespread sense that our political and social system has serious inadequacies.

We can no longer continue to operate on the basis of reacting to crises, counting on crash programs and the expenditure of huge sums of money to solve our problems. We have got to understand and project present trends, to take command of the forces that are emerging, to extend our freedom and wellbeing as citizens and the future of other nations and peoples in the world.

Because of the complexity and interdependence of issues facing America and the world today, the Commission has organized its work into six panels, which emphasize the interrelationships of critical choices rather than treating each one in isolation.

The six panels are:

Panel I: Energy and its Relationship to Ecology, Economics and World Stability;

Panel II: Food, Health, World Population and Quality of Life;

Panel III: Raw Materials, Industrial Development, Capital Formation, Employment and World Trade;

Panel IV: International Trade and Monetary Systems, Inflation and the Relationships Among Differing Economic Systems;

Panel V: Change, National Security and Peace;

Panel VI: Quality of Life of Individuals and Communities in the U.S.A.

The Commission assigned, in these areas, more than 100 authorities to prepare expert studies in their fields of special competence. The Commission's work has been financed by The Third Century Corporation, a New York not-for-profit organization. The corporation has received contributions from individuals and foundations to advance the Commission's activities.

The Commission is determined to make available to the public these background studies and the reports of those panels which have completed their deliberations. The background studies are the work of the authors and do not necessarily represent the views of the Commission or its members.

This volume is one of the series of volumes the Commission will publish in the belief that it will contribute to the basic thought and foresight America will need in the future.

WILLIAM J. RONAN
Acting Chairman
Commission on Critical Choices
for Americans

Members of the Commission

THE HONORABLE JOHN RHODES
   Minority Leader
   United States House of Representatives

Acting Chairman

WILLIAM J. RONAN
   Chairman, Port Authority of New York
   and New Jersey

Members

IVAN ALLAN, JR.
   Former Mayor of Atlanta, Georgia

MARTIN ANDERSON
   Senior Fellow, Hoover Institution of War,
   Revolution and Peace, Stanford University

ROBERT O. ANDERSON
   Chairman, Atlantic Richfield Company

MRS. W. VINCENT ASTOR
   Philanthropist and Author

WILLIAM O. BAKER
   President, Bell Telephone Laboratories, Inc.

DANIEL J. BOORSTIN
   Senior Historian, Smithsonian Institution

NORMAN ERNEST BORLAUG
   Agronomist; Nobel Peace Prize, 1970

ERNEST L. BOYER
   Chancellor, State University of New York

GUIDO CALABRESI
   John Thomas Smith Professor of Law,
   Yale University

LEO CHERNE
Executive Director, Research Institute
of America, Inc.

JOHN S. FOSTER, JR.
Vice President for Energy Research
and Development, TRW, Inc.

LUTHER H. FOSTER
President, Tuskegee Institute

NANCY HANKS
Chairman, National Endowment for the Arts

BELTON KLEBERG JOHNSON
Texas Rancher and Businessman

CLARENCE B. JONES
Former Editor and Publisher,
The New York Amsterdam News

JOSEPH LANE KIRKLAND
Secretary—Treasurer, AFL-CIO

JOHN H. KNOWLES, M.D.
President, Rockefeller Foundation

DAVID S. LANDES
Leroy B. Williams Professor of History
and Political Science, Harvard University

MARY WELLS LAWRENCE
Chairman and Chief Executive Officer,
Wells, Rich, Greene, Inc.

SOL M. LINOWITZ
Senior Partner of Coudert Brothers

EDWARD J. LOGUE
Former President and Chief Executive Officer,
New York State Urban Development Corporation

CLARE BOOTHE LUCE
Author; former Ambassador
and Member of Congress

PAUL WINSTON McCRACKEN
Professor of Business Administration,
University of Michigan

DANIEL PATRICK MOYNIHAN
The United States Representative to
the United Nations

BESS MYERSON
Former Commissioner of Consumer Affairs,
City of New York

WILLIAM S. PALEY
Chairman of the Board
Columbia Broadcasting System

RUSSELL W. PETERSON
Chairman, Council on Environmental
Quality

WILSON RILES
Superintendent of Public Instruction,
State of California

LAURANCE S. ROCKEFELLER
Environmentalist and Businessman

OSCAR M. RUEBHAUSEN
Partner, Debevoise, Plimpton, Lyons
and Gates, New York

GEORGE P. SHULTZ
Executive Vice President
Bechtel Corporation

JOSEPH C. SWIDLER
Partner, Leva, Hawes, Symington, Martin
& Oppenheimer
Former Chairman, Federal Power Commission

EDWARD TELLER
Senior Research Fellow, Hoover Institution
on War, Revolution and Peace,
Stanford University

ARTHUR K. WATSON*
Former Ambassador to France

MARINA VON NEUMANN WHITMAN
Distinguished Public Service Professor
of Economics, University of Pittsburgh

CARROLL L. WILSON
Professor, Alfred P. Sloan
School of Management,
Massachusetts Institute of Technology

GEORGE D. WOODS
Former President, World Bank

Members of the Commission served on the panels. In addition, others assisted
the panels.

BERNARD BERELSON
Senior Fellow
President Emeritus
The Population Council

C. FRED BERGSTEN
Senior Fellow
The Brookings Institution

ORVILLE G. BRIM, JR.
President
Foundation for Child Development

LESTER BROWN
President
Worldwatch Institute

LLOYD A. FREE
President
Institute for International Social Research

*Deceased

J. GEORGE HARRAR
Former President
Rockefeller Foundation

WALTER LEVY
Economic Consultant

PETER G. PETERSON
Chairman of the Board
Lehman Brothers

ELSPETH ROSTOW
Dean, Division of General and Comparative Studies
University of Texas

WALT W. ROSTOW
Professor of Economics and History
University of Texas

SYLVESTER L. WEAVER
Communications Consultant

JOHN G. WINGER
Vice President
Energy Economics Division
Chase Manhattan Bank

Preface

The equitable distribution of our resources will pose critical choices for this country as we move into the last decades of this century. Increasing world population growth and lagging food production will doubtless mean complex and painful decisions for us as a people and new challenges for us as the world's leading food producer. The Commission's Panel II—Food, Health, World Population and Quality of Life—asked Michael S. Teitelbaum, Harrison Brown, James L. Draper, Jonathan Elam, and Stewart Bledsoe to consider several of these choices. Traditionally, the United States has willingly expended its abundant agricultural production to feed the world's hungry in times of need, but today's population growth and other factors now overwhelm our ability to be the world's baker.

Moreover, and more than ever before, the American people are questioning a founding belief of this country that universal growth is unquestionably good and the more growth the better. We do not want to see growth abandoned—and the peoples of less developed countries yearn for the rewards of industrialization. It is a question of how we grow—and harmonization may be the key. The Commission's Panel I—Energy and Its Relationship to Ecology, Economics and World Stability—commissioned William K. Reilly and Robert Cahn of the Conservation Foundation to review the uses of our land and the environmental ethic of our national heritage.

Perhaps energy and the environment can and properly ought to be allies, as Henry L. Diamond suggests in his essay, through "old-fashioned conservation," which "advocated wise use of resources and wasting not." In all of these critical areas we are witnessing the emergence of new values for growth. This emergence brings with it an unparalleled opportunity to move through these values toward more fruitful and more enjoyable lives for us all.

W.J.R.

Contents

List of Figures

List of Tables

Introduction

Sudden freedom from historic constraints has often produced excess. The lottery winner, the college student just out of his parents' home, the school boy athlete who turns millionaire when he signs his pro contract, the obscure official who emerges from the coup as head of state: all have sometimes found their earlier experience, bounded by constraints now removed, an insufficient guide to the choices now suddenly available. They have often responded to their new freedom by going on a spree.

When historians look back on the twentieth century, they may conclude that the United States and much of the Western world were having just such a spree. Urban residents, freed by the automobile from the constraints of earlier transportation technology, moved outward from city centers. Millions of consumers, freed by a powerful industrial economy from age old economic constraints, were able to command an unprecedented array of goods and services.

The new millionaire or head of state may continue his spree for years, even decades, ending it only when a new constraint is established or an old one reimposed. The over-age prize fighter may find that his money has run out. The head of state may not survive the next coup or the next election.

Many people today believe that new constraints are about to impose themselves on the economy and lifestyle of the United States. For several years pollution was the most widely discussed of these anticipated constraints, particularly after dramatic projections of the Club of Rome report, *Limits to Growth.* Today, energy appears to be the most fundamental constraint. While some observers see the immediate energy shortage as principally a political problem created by the cartel of oil exporters, others—including the students of net energy—see energy as likely to impose fundamental, long-term constraints. Still other possible constraints are frequently discussed in the press: shortages of food and other resources, the "dying" of the oceans, the melting of polar ice caps, disruption of the protective ozone layer that is vital to humans.

It is possible that the United States is destined to continue its twentieth century spree until one or another of these constraints clearly imposes itself upon us. Americans were "people of plenty" even before the twentieth century, and the material prosperity of the past few decades appears to have reinforced our materialism. Expectations have risen to unprecedented heights, and it may well be that only external constraints can rein them in.

This is not, however, the only possibility. Experience with new freedom has often brought maturity and a new awareness of truths temporarily forgotten. After a time on his own, the young adult may impose, from within, many of the same constraints that his parents once imposed upon him. The millionaire may find that material pleasures, once so exciting, are ultimately less rewarding than spiritual satisfactions.

There is a profoundly important question whether we as a nation, and that presumably includes governments as well as individuals within it, are reaching a stage of maturity at which we want to turn away from some of the materialism that has characterized this century. A growing number of people, notably among the young, seem already to have made such a change in their personal values, and many others recognize that the good material life is not enough, is somehow unfulfilling.

Indeed, it is at least possible that the power of the environmental movement represents, at least as much as a concern with purity of air and water, a mature belief that we must move beyond consumption to find fulfillment. When environmentalists seem almost to welcome reports that the oceans may be dying or that pollution is causing cancer, it may be because they see such natural disasters as the only forces strong enough to cause policy changes that they believe are dictated by morality or ethics.

Some of these policy changes may present the biggest choice of all. "A society that is declining materially may be ascending spiritually,"[1] said Toynbee. William Ophuls, a political scientist at Yale University, states the vision this way:

A very good life—in fact, an affluent life by historic standards—can be lived without the profligate use of resources that characterizes our civilization. A sophisticated and ecologically sound technology, using solar power and other renewable resources, could bring us a life of simple sufficiency that would allow the full expression of the human potential. Having chosen such a life, rather than having had it forced on us, we might find it had its own richness.[2]

The greatest obstacle to value adaptation appears to be the high material expectations of the American people. Observers are suggesting that those expectations are already unrealistically high. The ending or slowing of the twentieth century spree, whether voluntary or forced, could render them even more unrealistic.

The implications of any such adjustment will be far-reaching. There will, surely, be intensified demands for equality of sacrifices—if only to demonstrate that downward revision of expectations is not merely the result of scheming by profiteers, known or unknown. The optimistic belief that our economy already has power to satisfy virtually any level of expectation—and the corollary belief that shortfalls represent a "rip-off," a willful failure to use that power equitably—will not be put to rest without persuasive proof of its inaccuracy.

Can our democratic institutions provide the needed proof? Can they provide the leadership needed to end the spree voluntarily or even to respond in an orderly fashion to constraints imposed from without? The answer is unclear for there is little experience to guide us.

We are concerned, however, about lack of confidence in the institutions that profoundly influence people's lives. The large corporate producers, and the large governments that alone have power to control them, too often seem equally remote and unresponsive to individual thoughts and feelings. "They," not "we," make most of the important decisions. This alienation may be inherently unacceptable. It is surely unacceptable when "they" have not succeeded in winning and retaining the respect of those whose lives they affect.

Five of the chapters in this volume consider world population growth and the interrelated problems of food production and agricultural policy in the United States. Another examines our use of land in urban and rural settings.

The seventh, and opening, chapter, by Conservation Foundation writer-in-residence Robert Cahn, considers environmental ethics. This ethical stance, now increasingly accepted, embodies the growing awareness that responsibility for a better environment cannot be left to government alone, but that all citizens, in their work and in their private lives, must take responsibility to assure that their actions do not contribute to upsetting the balance of nature or of preventing their neighbor from having the opportunity for a better quality of life. To apply environmental ethics will bring difficult choices to all of us in all walks of life and will possibly include the need for changing values and lifestyles and reappraising the economic impact and costs of our decisions.

Notes

1. Toynbee, Arnold, *London Observer*, April 14, 1974.
2. Ophuls, William, *Environmental Politics*, edited by Stuart S. Nagel (Praeger, 1974).

I

The Environmental Ethic

Robert Cahn

Part I. The Need for an Environmental Ethic

For two centuries this nation has been living off its rich natural heritage and often mistreating the earth and its resources. Today many Americans are recognizing that whether or not they apply ethical standards to the use of land, water, and air constitutes a significant national issue.

Population and technological growth, accompanied by an ever-higher standard of living, have now placed excessive demands and stresses on our natural environmental systems. Many Americans have come to acknowledge that what they thought was endless abundance now presents significant prospects of scarcity. The resources that have been treated so cavalierly are now in dire need of responsible treatment. And the goal to which all our efforts were directed—a satisfying and higher quality of life—is becoming increasingly elusive.

Dickens' words could be used to describe our status: "It was the best of times, it was the worst of times," he wrote in *A Tale of Two Cities*. On one hand, we in the United States enjoy "the best of times." We can point to an exceptionally high average family income, increasing life span, new opportunities for women and minorities. Appreciation of the arts, interest in books, and awareness of nature have expanded and broadened among the populace. Technology has filled the marketplace with time- and work-saving conveniences. Work is safer, the work day is shorter, and more time is available for leisure

---

This material is treated in greater detail in a forthcoming book by the author on *A Search for an Environmental Ethic*.

1

activities. Privacy, which we value highly, is available to most people. We have a strong Constitutional government and process. The great majority of families have an automobile and the mobility it affords. Air travel has further increased mobility. Television has brought the wide world and outer space into the humblest dwelling and broadened the scope of experience for people in even the remotest places.

Yet, it could also be considered "the worst of times." We have been slowly choking off our vital lifelines. Despite progress in combating pollution, the air is fouled with toxic substances and smog, oceans are threatened with oil and waste discharges, the fuel for home, industry, and transport has become scarce and expensive, with a bleak long-term outlook. Even drinking water, which we thought we had made pure and safe, is now suspected of causing disease in a number of urban areas.

The automobile, for all its liberating qualities, has led to urban and suburban sprawl, traffic congestion, noise, and air pollution. We lose more than a million acres of forest and meadow, marsh and wetlands, hill and dale each year to development of highways, airports, subdivisions or strip mining of coal.[1] Since the Pilgrims arrived, 47 species of mammals and birds have become extinct, 109 species are currently threatened with extinction, and more than 2,000 plants are on the endangered list.[2] One in three marriages now ends in divorce;[3] one in five Americans moves each year.[4] Faith in institutions declines, respect for government deteriorates. Some affluent Americans tell pollsters they are getting more satisfaction out of life. Yet signs are evident all around that people feel a vague and sometimes sharp dissatisfaction with their work and with life itself, and that yesterday's rising expectations are for much of the nation still unfulfilled.

Ethics Questioned

There is reason to question whether the traditional means for shaping values and ethics—family, religion, education, community—have as much influence as they had in earlier times; and people are searching for new ways to shape those ethics. Great as the need may be to restore our general ethical base, however, there is an accompanying need to expand ethics in new directions, especially toward a sense of responsibility for preservation or enhancement of the environment. For while the environment is not presently perceived as a survival issue with priority equal to that of food, shelter, and population control, it is a basic issue involving the condition and potential of the world on which we and our successors will live.

"There is as yet no ethic dealing with man's relation to land and to the animals and plants which grow upon it," wrote Aldo Leopold a quarter of a century ago in presenting a philosophical and practical base for consideration of environmental ethics.[5] Recognizing that the individual is a member of a community of interdependent parts, he concluded that "the land ethic simply enlarges the boundaries of the community to include soils, waters, plants, and animals, or collectively: the land. . . . In short, a land ethic changes the role of *Homo sapiens* from conqueror of the land-community to plain member and citizen of it. It implies respect for his fellow-members, and also respect for the community as such."[6]

Few of us understand or accept responsibility for the way our decisions and actions may be affecting the environment of our neighbor, our community, our state, our nation, the world and the planet. We are a people who abide by law. The majority accept the responsibilities of political citizenship; we vote, pay taxes, obey laws. But it is a rare individual who considers environmental responsibility, environmental citizenship.

Individual Responsibility

All too often we leave responsibility for a better environment to government. While this has resulted in much environmental betterment in recent years, it does not replace the need for participation by every citizen. Federal, state, and local antipollution laws are imposing a degree of corporate environmental responsibility. The National Environmental Policy Act of 1969, and similar laws in a number of states, have required governmental decisionmakers to assess the environmental impacts of their actions and consider alternate courses of action.

Concern for the public good has occasionally been given precedence over the rights of property owners to develop land. States and localities have enacted restrictive laws and ordinances. In a few states, special laws such as those outlawing throw-away cans or bottles have resulted in reduced litter and reuse of bottles, thus conserving resources. Still another method, as yet virtually untried for encouraging environmental responsibility, is the enactment of tax subsidies or penalties.

Laws can guide individual responsibility, but "environmental citizenship" involves and requires much more if we are to improve the environment on a permanent basis. The great potential resource of environmental citizenship lies in widespread acceptance in environmental matters of the American tradition of individual action and personal responsibility far beyond the legally established minimum.

Toward a Definition of an Environmental Ethic

Like wind, an ethic is noticed by its effects. The environmental ethic shows up in many aspects of daily living. If we are environmentally ethical, we look not only to immediate effects of actions, but beyond, to the wide-ranging, long-term effects of our actions upon the land, waters, and all forms of life, and especially on our neighbors with whom we share the natural resources. Implicit here is an awareness of the wholeness of life in which everything is related to everything else. When we begin to see ourselves as participants in an evolutionary process, then a fundamentally new understanding of human activity begins to emerge.

The ecological system, from the biotic community of a flood plain to the interrelated complexities of a metropolis, depends partly on its web of interconnectiveness. It also depends on diversity to achieve stability. In a healthy ecological system each organism fills a niche. What one organism doesn't use, another may live on: strengthening the whole. Each part of the system has evolved in such a way that it can cope with natural fluctuations. A failure in one part of the web of life can affect the entire biotic community. The community can often adjust to minor changes. But if a key member is removed, the whole system suffers, and may be seriously disrupted for years or even irreversibly altered. Humankind is the member of this web of life with unique abilities to alter it for better or worse, as well as the one member having conscience and the ability to reason.

Citizens imbued with the environmental ethic would view themselves as part of a universe governed by nature and social values. They would respect nature and the natural processes on which all life depends, including their own. Individuals practicing environmental citizenship would try to assure that their actions and the effects of the actions would not impair the health of other species or their own. Nor would they poison the land or water or the atmosphere. And they would be sensitive and responsive to minimizing the impact of their actions on the stability, variety, and balance of their ecosystem.

Those who are environmentally ethical also would realize they cannot live for the present moment only, but must consider the effects of their actions on their children and on succeeding generations. Those who inherit the land, water, sky, and all the natural world should bear some responsibility for stewardship. Aldo Leopold once wrote that citizens must "examine each question in terms of what is ethically and esthetically right, as well as what is economically expedient. A thing is right when it tends to preserve the integrity, stability, and beauty of the biotic community. It is wrong when it tends otherwise."[7]

Some may question this attitude as being overly concerned with the biotic community to the neglect of human social needs. Yet Leopold considered man a part of the biotic community. He was suggesting that we cannot judge right and wrong only in terms of immediate consequences and self-interest, but should judge whether or not an action is going to contribute to the balance of an entire ecosystem.

Living by the Ethic

Living by an environmental ethic does not imply that all must undergo a radical change of lifestyle immediately, or go back three centuries to the rigors of an independent, self-contained style of living. Some people may want to get away from the city to rural living, and have a simpler lifestyle or live in the city and give up their automobiles.

Such a lifestyle change is not practical for everyone, and may not be the best course of action for most people. However, models such as those in the Club of Rome study, *Limits to Growth*[8] —even though controversial as to techniques and forecasts—have focused attention on the finite nature of resources and food and the impacts of population growth and pollution which head us toward a day of reckoning unless some changes are made in the ever-increasing demands of mankind. The projection of "limits" has at least given many citizens cause to reassess their own individual and collective actions as they have impact on available resources.

Actions, on the part of individuals, that are small, environmentally aware and responsible have a cumulative effect that will be felt by the marketplace, by the political system, and by the ecosystem itself. As was demonstrated during the 1973-74 energy crisis, individual actions such as turning the thermostat down in homes and offices, walking or using public transportation or car pooling instead of driving, reducing the number and intensity of lights, had the cumulative effect of reducing energy consumption significantly (if temporarily), thereby reducing in that crisis the aggregate demand upon a limited resource.

Leadership in this shift to more environmentally ethical lifestyles has come from young people. Many of them have started to practice what some of their elders preach. The young have discerned that material accumulation fails to bring either satisfaction or security. Many have experimented with growing their own food—organically—and started communes in rural and urban areas. Many have delved into Eastern lifestyles such as practiced in Zen Buddhism, or have been attracted to other newer Eastern philosophies and groups which deemphasize materialism and have lifestyles frugal in the use of resources and in harmony with nature.

The search for a simpler and more environmentally harmonious lifestyle has not been confined to the young, however. Many adults, including corporate leaders, have learned from their children or from their own dissatisfaction with their lives, the need for a new value structure and a desire for a simpler lifestyle. Some adults are learning crafts so they can leave the assembly line. Many are moving back to small rural communities where they seek to be less dependent on outside organizations, governments, and the total economic system for all their wants and necessities. Others are finding ways to simplify their lifestyle while remaining in the city.

Different ethics will be dominant in different times. At times, an individualistic survival ethic has dominated in the United States. At other times in the history of our country, the work ethic has prevailed. At present, an ethic of excessive consumption dominates.

The ethics of the industrial or technological age have emphasized competition, mastery of technology, and increasing speed, efficiency, and bigness. The priority has been placed on systems or machines that work efficiently, make money, and increase production. Spreading wastes with abandon and carelessly damaging the health of workers, customers, and neighbors have all been tolerated under previous ethical codes. These were unfortunate costs incidental to what were viewed as the general benefits of material growth.

This long-dominant Western viewpoint is symbolized by the statement of the influential British economist, John Maynard Keynes, who wrote in 1930: "For at least another hundred years we must pretend to ourselves and to everyone that fair is foul and foul is fair; for foul is useful and fair is not. Avarice and usury and precaution must be our gods for a little longer still. For only they can lead us out of the tunnel of economic necessity into daylight."[9]

A radically different view has been taken by another British economist, E.F. Schumacher. He sees our obsession with technology and materialism and our overly constricted view of its world as the basic moral issue. He believes we are getting warnings not just from the downtrodden and oppressed but from the environment itself. Schumacher writes:

We pose questions to the universe by what we do, . . . and the universe, by its response, informs us of whether our actions fit into its laws or not. Small transgressions evoke limited or mild responses; large transgressions evoke general, threatening, and possibly violent responses. The very universality of the environmental crisis indicates the universality of our transgressions . . . what is most needed today is a revision of the ends which all our efforts are meant to serve. And this implies that above all else we need the development of a lifestyle which accords to material things their proper, legitimate place, which is secondary and not primary.[10]

Conflict with Economics

The conflict between the environmental ethic and the traditional economic system raises the most vexing issues. Some economists, such as Professor Milton Friedman of the University of Chicago, oppose allowing environmental or social responsibility to be considered in corporate decision-making when not specifically required. "There is one and only one social responsibility of business—to use its resources and engage in activities to increase its profits," Professor Friedman has written.[11] He also has stated that, "Any businessman who boasts to the public that he has been using corporate funds to exercise a social responsibility should be regarded as asking for an investigation by the Anti-trust Division of the Justice Department."[12] But he tempers this remark somewhat by saying that money spent for a social consideration can be justified if it is in the interests of the corporation.

Banker Louis B. Lundborg, a present director and former chairman of the board of the Bank of America, argues strongly that corporate leadership should be responsive to environmental and social concerns: "Those in corporate life are going to be expected to do things for the good of society, just to earn their franchise, their corporate right to exist."[13] Corporate social involvement, he says, is clearly an obligation. "The corporation has to earn its right to exist and to function—and it has to earn that right all over again every single day of its life."[14]

Debating over corporate social responsibility is nonsense, Lundborg adds. "Environmental and other social problems should get *at least* as much corporate attention as production, sales, and finance. The quality of life in its total meaning is, in the final reckoning, the only justification for any corporate activity."[15]

Difficult Choices

An environmental ethic, like all ethics, results from discovering for ourselves what our role is in the ecosystem and what that role demands. Ethics are present in us as precepts that impel a certain kind of action or response. They can become so ingrained in consciousness that actions appear to come from instinct or habit, rather than from any formal code of ethics.

It is important that the environmental ethic not be left on the shelf to be taken down and dusted off for use only after work or when otherwise convenient. It should undergird all actions at all times, for the company executive or professional worker or blue-collar laborer on the job or off, by the educator and student at school, by the civic worker, or by the environmental activist, who needs to be guided by this ethic as much as anyone.

This presents the individual with many obstacles and difficult choices. A lawyer, for instance, may feel obligated to the system of justice and the legal code of ethics which do not include consideration of an environmental ethic in relationships with clients. An architect might raise the point: If I practice an environmental ethic, and my competitor does not, I will lose business. A banker might say: I could not possibly use environmental concerns in my investment or loan policy, because it is not my own money. Or corporate officials might believe that their responsibility to the shareholders, stockholders or employees is to make as much profit as possible, and that following an environmental ethic would conflict with their more immediate responsibility.

Sociologist Abraham Maslow, in his book *Motivation and Personality*,[16] set forth a hierarchy of needs. He pointed out that the "higher" needs—belongingness, love, esteem and self-actualization—cannot be met until the lower ones, such as food, air, water, safety and security are satisfied. The environmental issues now being raised, and the degree to which they are given priority, may be an indication of where our needs are in the hierarchy, and could be telling us what kind of a society we are, where we are going, and what we need to do to get there.

Part II. The Emergence of an Environmental Ethic

Sixty-seven years ago, President Theodore Roosevelt hosted a White House Conference on the Conservation of Natural Resources. For three days, the nation's governors, most of the cabinet and the Supreme Court, and a thousand national citizen leaders discussed conservation and natural resource problems. Given the keynote remarks of the president, this could have been the start of our nation's adherence to a new environmental ethic. His remarks appear remarkably relevant to today's problems.

We have become great in a material sense because of the lavish use of our resources, and we have just reason to be proud of our growth. But the time has come to inquire seriously what will happen when our forests are gone, when the coal, the iron, the oil, and the gas are exhausted, when the soils shall have been still further impoverished and washed into the streams, polluting the rivers, denuding the fields, and obstructing navigation. These questions do not relate only to the next century or to the next generation. One distinguishing characteristic of really civilized men is foresight; we have to, as a nation, exercise foresight for this nation in the future.[17]

The president warned that the natural resources were in danger of exhaustion if wasteful methods of exploiting them continued. He spoke of the average man who lives in a big city getting out of touch with nature and losing his sense of his dependence upon nature at the same time he was increasing his demands on it. He spoke of the American settlers and pioneers who were not aware of any duty to posterity in dealing with the resources.

In the past we have admitted the right of the individual to injure the future of the Republic for his own present profit. In fact there has been a good deal of a demand for unrestricted individualism, for the right of the individual to injure the future of all of us for his own temporary and immediate profit. The time has come for a change. As a people we have the right and the duty, second to none other but the right and duty of obeying the moral law, of requiring and doing justice, to protect ourselves and our children against the wasteful development of our natural resources, whether that waste is caused by the actual destruction of such resources or by making them impossible of development hereafter.[18]

Unfortunately, Mr. Roosevelt's fine rhetoric and the White House Conference did not turn around the values and ethics of the nation. His chief advisor for conservation, Gifford Pinchot, worked hard to promote "wise use" of resources, led in the expansion of federal forest reserves, encouraged the elimination of wasteful practices, and advanced other conservation ideas. But President Roosevelt had other issues and Congress had higher priorities, and no organized follow-through to the conference in new legislation took place.

Early America

The environmental ethic, subordinated by the survival, expansion, and utilitarian ethics which were dominant in the Colonial, Federal, and Western Expansion periods of American history, has been a long time evolving.

In early America, the new settlers' values and attitudes toward nature clashed with those of the native American Indians. The Indians' religious creed gave them a concept of wholeness which led to a sense of stewardship, of reverence and respect for the land and for nature. They lived then in comparative harmony with the natural environment, for the land was seen as a part of them.

The colonists brought with them a radically different set of ethical values. They felt the practical need to conquer the land and make it productive to support their civilization and growing population. In line with their Christian tradition, they believed in man's dominion over nature and that nature was to be subdued by man so that all of creation might glorify its Creator. Their radical monotheism together with their increasing understanding of natural laws had eliminated from nature much of its mystery, as well as its sacredness. Their political system provided that land could be owned and developed as needed. And when they found a harsh wilderness before them, instead of the friendly land they had anticipated, they necessarily viewed the land and its wildness as something to be conquered and subjugated.

But their European heritage also included seeds of an environmental ethic which had been slowly germinating over the centuries. Many early settlers practiced limited forms of conservation. In some areas for instance, restrictions were placed on deer hunting.[19] William Penn decreed that for every five acres of land cleared, one must be left forested.[20] Thomas Jefferson and many of his peers practiced a benign control over property and nature, seeking to assure continued productivity by good land practices and by developing an esthetically pleasing and orderly landscape. They also saw the land as more than a utilitarian source of goods and wealth; property ownership was regarded as conferring dignity and status, giving the owner not only control of the land but also responsibility and a stake in his country.

The God-fearing settlers' views were also shaped by centuries of religious tradition. The Old Testament story of creation—with God giving man "dominion" over all the earth—can be interpreted, as it has by some Biblical scholars, as implying stewardship, instead of exploitation. This idea of stewardship is brought out in passages such as that in the book of Ezekial, where the prophet admonishes shepherds "that do feed themselves! Should not the shepherds feed the flock?"[21]

The Golden Rule, as given by Jesus: "As ye would that men should do to you, do ye also to them likewise,"[22] is, of course, a basic underpinning in the practice of an environmental ethic. And fifteen hundred years ago, Saint Benedict of Nursia preached and practiced how to manage the land and how to have a harmonious but practical relationship between man and nature, while later, Saint Francis of Assisi taught reverence for nature. The Eastern religions and civilizations also preached a reverence for nature. But their practices, like those of Western peoples, led to devastation of forests, erosion of the land, and extinction of much of the wildlife.

The Age of Exploration in Europe, from the sixteenth through early nineteenth centuries, had considerable effect on the American colonists and early settlers. It was the time of the development and growth of modern science, of inventions, and of worldwide explorations which climaxed in industrialized Western society. Many of the scientist-philosophers of the age sought to redefine the world in moral as well as material terms, espousing man's control over nature. However, the nature philosophy of the new Americans was also influenced by two other traditions: man's responsibility for nature, held by the natural scientists of the seventeenth century, and the later view of respect and reverence for nature, set forth by the writers, musicians, and artists of the eighteenth and early nineteenth centuries.

The prediction by the Polish astronomer Copernicus, in 1543, that the earth was in orbit around the sun challenged the existing Christian explanations of man's relationship to the world: the traditional belief in the earth as God's gift to man, and of man as the center of the universe. However, Copernicus and his contemporaries were devoutly religious men who saw no conflict between their scientific research and their Christian concepts of a world design and divine order. Their basic Christian premise stressed that man's task was to understand and unravel God's natural order. They believed that through their scientific inquiries they were participating in God's creation by bringing more order to God's design. "The empire of man over things depends wholly on the arts and sciences," explained Francis Bacon. With the growing acceptance of these beliefs and attitudes, the scientist-philosophers attempted to bring the natural world under man's domination.

Galileo envisioned a material world open to quantification, abstraction, and ordering. Galileo's philosophy of a material world composed of strictly lifeless molecules furthered the new scientific method, which valued "physical properties" over the "life qualities" of the natural world.

The mechanistic concept of nature developed by the French mathematician and philosopher, René Descartes, meant that nature was describable in materialistic terms and was of no intrinsic value. Nature thus existed exclusively for the use and benefit of man. Descartes suggested that God was the machine maker and the fashioner of the earth, the body of man and all plant and animal life. The earth and its workings were likened to a clock, of predictable operation and tick-tock precision, and which operated according to a predetermined Divine plan to meet man's needs. In a utilitarian tone, Descartes declared, "There is nothing created from which we cannot derive some use." Thus, according to the attitudes and concepts of the classical scientist, nature was given value only if it had a value for man.

The life sciences, or natural sciences, which emerged in the seventeenth century viewed nature differently. They provided an optimistic view of man and nature, although they had only a minor influence at the time. The life scientists maintained basic religious beliefs similar to those of the classical scientists in respect to faith in a world design and divine order, an order designed for man's benefit and use. But their studies in geography, natural history, and related sciences gave them a view of the wholeness of nature, its interrelationships and its inner life. They believed this to be a proof of God's wisdom. The natural scientists accepted nature as having intrinsic value and held man to be responsible for nature. According to the seventeenth century naturalist John Ray, man's growing knowledge of the nature of life and the environment would lead to the improvement of man and society.

Concerning the different basic beliefs expounded by the classical scientists and life scientists of the seventeenth century, Ray wrote: "It is a generally received opinion, that all this visible world was created for Man; that Man is the End of Creation; as if there were no other end of any creature, but some way or other serviceable to man . . . yet wise men now-adays think otherwise . . . that creatures are made to enjoy themselves as well as to serve us."[2 3]

While the classical scientists probed the parts, actions and interactions of the physical world and the natural scientists concentrated on its interrelationships and wholeness, their respective findings contributed to attitudes which valued the utilitarian rather than the esthetic aspects of the natural world. Scientific knowledge came to symbolize the promise of a better way of life and brighter future for mankind and society. And the classical scientist-philosophers were mainly responsible for laying the foundations which spawned the industrial revolution, with man shaping his universe to his design.

On the other hand, the roots of the modern environmental movement can be traced to the literature, music, and paintings of the eighteenth and nineteenth century Romanticists, including the Frenchman Rousseau and Englishmen Blake, Wordsworth, and Shelley. The Romantics found the new scientific attitude toward nature unacceptable in that it attempted to sever the long and rich man-nature relationship. The Romantic idea was a rebellion against the artificiality and emptiness of the mechanical view of nature. In an attempt to continue the traditions of Saint Francis of Assisi, Dante, and Milton, the Romantic movement glorified the living landscape in terms of its natural beauty, variety, and richness of life. Man was seen as a part of nature, vulnerable to nature's inner spirit and qualities, and entrusted with nature's care. According to the Romantic philosophy, man and nature shared, in dynamic relationships, common qualities. "Everything that lives," said William Blake, "lives not alone, nor of itself." The common qualities of man and nature included colors, sensations, and beauty as well as creativity, imagination, and harmony. This belief is shared in the simple, yet powerful verse of William Blake:

To see a World in a Grain of Sand
And a Heaven in a Wild Flower,
Hold infinity in the palm of your hand
And Eternity in an hour.

Jean-Jacques Rousseau, landscape painter and philosopher, enthusiastically called to his countrymen to return to a simpler, more primitive way of life. In response to Europe's growing acceptance of the classical scientific way of thinking and acting, Rousseau's philosophy reflected the desire to begin the human experience all over again. The new beginning would exalt the permanence and integrity of nature. "Nature," explained Rousseau, "never deceives us; it is always we who deceive ourselves." In advocating a new and better society, Rousseau believed that man's spiritual improvement would grow from man's oneness with nature.

English poet William Wordsworth conversed with the trees, the mountains, the sea . . . "my mind hath looked upon the speaking face of the earth." In nature he experienced the realities of life. He vehemently objected to the uniformity and dehumanizing order of modern science. Wordsworth believed in an open man-nature dialogue. "Come forth into the light of things. Let Nature be your teacher," he wrote. Wordsworth berated the urban environment of city life, and he encouraged his fellow Englishmen to go out and meet with nature on her grounds, to find enjoyment, life and beauty in the natural landscape. The nature philosophy of his poetry showed how the love of nature leads to the love of man:

One impulse from a vernal wood
may teach you more of man,
Of moral evil and of good,
Than all the sages can.

Percy Bysshe Shelley, English poet and contemporary of Wordsworth, embraced the promise of modern science. Science symbolized the future hope of man and society. However, like Wordsworth, Shelley refused to accept the materialistic and amoral side of science. His warning at the close of the age that science was advancing faster than the arts and humanities had little impact on England then close to becoming the world's first industrialized nation.

The industrial revolution and the intellectual reaction to it influenced the ethics of a young and growing America. The seeming abundance of natural resources encouraged practices that emphasized efficiency and speed of development, with little thought for the effects on the future of the land and resources. The quicker the development, the greater was the benefit and prosperity for the individual and for society. In this heady atmosphere, loggers stripped the forests with little or no regard for impact on the watershed, and gold miners destroyed mountainsides and river valleys with their hydraulic mining or dredging.

Nineteenth Century Efforts

Nevertheless, the environmental ethic stirred in the hearts of a few who foresaw the need to preserve for future generations. One small evidence is found in the journal of artist-explorer George Catlin, where he noted the possible extinction of the buffalo and their habitat in the wilderness of South Dakota. "Many are the rudenesses and wilds in nature's works which are destined to fall before the deadly axe and desolating hand of cultivating man," he wrote in his journal in 1832. And the buffalo and the wilderness might not disappear if they were

[by some great protecting policy of the government] preserved in their pristine beauty and wilderness, in a *magnificent* park, where the world could see for ages to come, the native Indian in his classic attire, galloping his wild horse . . . amid the fleeing herds of elks and buffaloes. What a beautiful and thrilling specimen for America to preserve and hold up to the view of her refined citizens and the world, in future ages! A *nation's park*, containing man and beast, in all the wild and freshness of their nature's beauty.[24]

When Congress established Yellowstone National Park, in 1872, as the world's first wild park to be set aside for the public, this revolutionary action went largely unnoticed. It resulted mainly from the lobbying of a few enthusiasts and the fact that no one else, least of all the miners, timber interests, and cattlemen, yet appreciated the potential of the land included in the park. It was inaccessible, hostile Indians were present, and the water power resource of the Yellowstone River was not recognized. In debate on the Yellowstone bill in 1871, a California senator argued against passage saying: "The natural curiosities there cannot be interfered with by anything that man can do. The geysers will remain, no matter where the ownership of the land may be, and I do not know why settlers should be excluded from a tract of land forty miles square, as I understand this to be, in the Rocky Mountains or any other place."[25]

Some efforts at conservation and preservation were evident during the nineteenth century in America, but it would be an exaggeration to see in them any real environmental movement. Under the impetus of Frederick Law Olmsted, New York authorized Central Park in 1853, and Olmsted designed and built it.[26] The City Beautiful movement of the 1880s and 1890s was an effort to bring the beauty of nature to the city. A number of states took early measures to protect their resources: California established Yosemite Valley as a state park in 1864,[27] and New York established the large Adirondack Forest Preserve in 1885, although the primary intent was to protect the watershed and water supply.[28]

The Swamp Land Act of 1849 may have been the first piece of national legislation aimed at wiser use of the land, although in today's view it would be considered anti-environment. The act was passed initially to control flood waters of the Mississippi River (and later was applied to other states), to protect farmland on the flood plain, and to aid in reclamation of swamplands thought to be worthless. The argument of its proponents was that if Congress could grant land for the building of canals, river improvements, and railroads, could it not give swamplands to the states for reclamation? In practice, however, the act produced little in the way of revitalizing the lands for the benefit of the people. Through fraud and mismanagement, much of the land wound up in the hands of large land investors. And little money accrued to the states from land sales to be used for building dams and reclamation projects.[29]

A landmark in the development of the environmental ethic was the publication in 1864 of George Perkins Marsh's book, *Man and Nature*.[30] While American minister to Turkey and to Italy, he saw European land devastated by bad farming and logging practices. He had seen similar conditions in his native Vermont, and sought to improve soil conservation practices in America. Marsh viewed the earth as a whole in which man was an intruder who failed to understand the laws of nature or the consequences of his actions, which threatened the balance of nature.

He cited specific examples of "soil exploitation and forest denudation." His illustration of the multiple effects of man's seemingly simple actions is classic. He writes of "the destruction of the mosquito, that feeds the trout, that preys on the May fly that destroys the eggs that hatch the salmon that pampers the epicure." He wrote: "Thus all nature is linked together by invisible bonds, and every organic creature however low, however feeble, however dependent, is necessary to the well-being of some other among the myriad of life with which the Creator has peopled the earth."[31] Marsh's book was a best seller in its day in America and in Europe. An optimist, he concluded that adherence to a better understanding of nature, the promise of science and technological innovations would enable man to redeem himself and restore the balance of nature.

Marsh was, in effect, the first American to write about the concepts of ecology. The English naturalist Charles Darwin, however, had outlined ecology's two basic ideas in *The Origin of Species* (1859). He described the fragile and complex interrelations of a natural community, and also the process of evolution in nature, which, he suggested, may apply to man. A German zoologist, Ernst Haeckel, coined the word "ecology" (Ocologie) in 1886, in a paper about a new science he said was concerned with "Nature's Economy." He derived the term from the Greek *oikos* meaning "household, or home or place to live" and he defined ecology as the "relation of the animal to its organic as well as its inorganic environment."[32] Haeckel used his new term to describe the way organisms interact or compete for food. (Today's popular usage applies the term ecology to the study of the relationships of all living things including man, to their environment.)

These concepts of the natural world as a living process sensitive to the actions of man, ran counter to the popular nineteenth century belief that the natural world was man's to possess and control.

American Transcendentalists

At the time of Marsh, the American version of Transcendentalism, led by Emerson and Thoreau, was gaining strength and followers. The American Transcendentalists emphasized immersing oneself in the world of nature, allowing one's unity with nature to lift one beyond ordinary materialistic values into spiritual awareness. To the American Transcendentalists, nature symbolized perfection and spiritual truth, and Emerson emphasized the power of "Nature" to heal men as well as heal itself. Thoreau, in his many writings, especially *Walden*, encouraged people to gain enjoyment from nature and learn its lessons about life. Thoreau may have written for the whole school of Transcendentalism when he wrote, "This curious world which we inhabit is more wonderful than it is convenient; more beautiful than it is useful; it is more to be admired than it is to be used."[33]

Along with Catlin, Thoreau urged preservation of wilderness and areas of great natural beauty as national parks and his phrase ... "In Wildness is the preservation of the World" has become a rallying cry of today's preservationists.

John Muir, while a student at the University of Wisconsin, was introduced to the Transcendentalist influence and became its leading far western prophet and exponent of wilderness values, especially those of California's Sierra Nevada. In addition to his reputation as a philosopher and writer on wilderness and preservation, Muir became a political activist and friend of presidents. He was active in the campaign to have Yosemite Valley and the surrounding mountains made into a national park in 1891, and in 1892 he helped to establish the Sierra Club to preserve wilderness values. He was host to President Theodore Roosevelt for a three-day camping trip in the Yosemite wilderness. Muir even encouraged the aging Emerson to visit Yosemite in 1883,[34] although he was disappointed when Emerson spent the night in a park hotel.

Utilitarian Conservation

In the latter half of the nineteenth century, the movement to control and protect natural resources gained strength. John Wesley Powell, who made the first descent of the Colorado River in 1869, and was the foremost explorer of the Grand Canyon, was an early sponsor of large federal reclamation and irrigation projects to bring water into the arid regions of the west. He became director of the U.S. Geological Survey two years after it was established in 1879.[35] Another early advocate of federal involvement in protection and development of natural resources was Carl Schurz, a secretary of the interior, who in 1877 advocated rational management of America's forests to save them for future generations.[36]

The leader of the movement, however, was Gifford Pinchot, who became the first American professional forester and who popularized the word "conservation" in 1905.[37] Pinchot became the principal exponent of the Progressive Conservation movement, which promoted wiser and more efficient use of the natural resources, especially forests and water, and designation of the natural resources as "public" resources. In 1898, Pinchot was named to head the new federal Forestry Division which became the U.S. Forest Service, and he was instrumental in setting aside millions of acres in a national forest system.[38] Production of timber on a sustained yield basis was the chief objective of the Forest Service. But its mission also included watershed management and wildlife habitat preservation.

The Conservation-Preservation Split

Muir and Pinchot were friends for a while, working for conservation and preservation from their own viewpoints: Pinchot with the utilitarian desires of wisest and best use of the resources, and Muir for the esthetic and ethical values of preservation of the land intact for present and future generations.

Soon after the turn of the century, however, they became bitter enemies over a long battle to build a reservoir in the pristine Hetch Hetchy valley of Yosemite National Park to supply water for San Francisco. Hetch Hetchy became a national issue which was finally decided in favor of Pinchot in 1913 when Congress, with the backing of Interior Secretary Franklin K. Lane, former attorney for the city of San Francisco, approved the Hetch Hetchy dam. The defeat broke Muir's heart, but not his spirit. He wrote that through Hetch Hetchy "the conscience of the whole country has been aroused from sleep."[39] And in one way, he did have the last word. Despite many attempts, no other dam has ever been built within a national park.

Twentieth Century Beginnings

In the first half of the twentieth century, the preservation and conservation activities grew along parallel lines. But as mid-century arrived, a growing convergence in goals lessened the strife and increased the opportunity for cooperation. Survival of new settlers and settlements along the frontiers of the country was no longer an overwhelming issue, and people could afford to relax their endeavors and give thought to social concerns.

On the preservation front in the early twentieth century, Congress passed the

Antiquities Act of 1906, permitting preservation as national monuments millions of acres of federal lands having unusual scientific, natural or historical significance.[40] The National Park Service was established in 1916 and expanded under the leadership of Stephen Mather and Horace Albright.[41] States protected natural areas as parks and forest reserves. Citizen organizations such as the National Audubon Society, the Save-the-Redwoods League, and the Wilderness Society were formed. Wilderness areas were set aside within national forests and given special protection against logging or development.

The conservation activities of the first half of the century included establishment of the U.S. Bureau of Reclamation and the building of many large dams and irrigation projects, and widespread flood control programs of the U.S. Army Corps of Engineers. Massive efforts at soil conservation were started, especially after the "dust bowl" experience of the early 1930s. These culminated in the establishment of the Soil Conservation Service of the Department of Agriculture. The huge Tennessee Valley Authority was formed to improve the environment of a large region through regional planning and multiple use of resources. The Taylor Grazing Act of 1934 gave the federal government control of use of public lands in the west.[42]

Serving both preservation and conservation objectives, efforts were made in wildlife management, including establishment of a system of national wildlife refuges and enactment of laws to regulate hunting, and to prevent import or export of endangered species.

Aldo Leopold's Vision

Aldo Leopold (1886-1948) made perhaps the most outstanding contribution to definition and promotion of environmental ethics during the first half of the century, although his influence is being felt more today than when he was alive. A graduate forester from Yale, Leopold was supervisor of the Carson National Forest in northern New Mexico. With a billion feet of timber and varied wildlife in the national forest, he became involved in problems of managing the land. He was a hunter and was at first an advocate of predator control. But on the nearby Arizona Kaibab Plateau in the 1920, the deer over-multiplied and tens of thousands starved to death following a conservation program that had sought to rid the area of all species that preyed upon the deer. Out of this experience, Leopold saw the need for a holistic, ecological approach to land management.

Leopold went on to become the leader in wildlife management. But even more important were his application of the principles of ecology and the philosophy of an environmental ethic that he developed over the next quarter century. Although a keen observer and appreciator of nature, he could not go along with the Transcendentalist concept of nearby Arizona Kaibab Plateau in the 1920s, the deer over-multiplied and to deny what could be learned from ecological inquiry. He also opposed conservation as it was then practiced because it placed responsibility for the resources not on the general public, but on professional managers with their strict use-minded purposes. From his first address on "the Conservation Ethic" in 1933, until his death in 1948, Leopold expanded his philosophy. A collection of his writings, *A Sand County Almanac*, published the year after his death, combines Thoreau-like observations of nature's web of life and what human beings can learn from it, with an expansion of ethics from the area of human relations to the interrelationship of the whole land community in which humans are participants.

A Sand County Almanac was not an automatic success, selling only a few thousand copies the first year. But it has become almost a "bible" to the newly-awakened environmentalists, and in 1973 sold 270,000 copies.[43]

Ethics first dealt with relations between individuals, Leopold wrote, then with integrating the individual into society, then with relating the social organization to the individual. He saw the emerging need for an ethic dealing with man's relation to the land and to the animals and plants which grow upon it. "Ethics are possibly a kind of community instinct in-the-making," he wrote.[44]

No important change in ethics was ever accomplished "without an internal change in our intellectual emphasis, loyalties, affections, and convictions," he wrote. "The proof that conservation has not yet touched these foundations of conduct lies in the fact that philosophy and religion have not yet heard of it. In our attempt to make conservation easy, we have made it trivial," he added.[45]

In his essay, *The Land Ethic*, he wrote that a system of conservation based solely on economic self-interest is hopelessly lopsided.

It tends to ignore and thus eventually to eliminate, many elements in the land community that lack commercial value, but that are (as far as we know) essential to its healthy functioning. It assumes, falsely, I think, that the economic parts of the biotic clock will function without the uneconomic parts. It tends to relegate to government many functions eventually too large, too complex, or too widely dispersed to be performed by government. An ethical obligation on the part of the private owner is the only visible remedy for these situations.[46]

Ecology, the Subversive Science

While Aldo Leopold was not a trained ecologist, his work did much to interpret for the lay public the growing science of ecology. Ecological studies developed in scope over the years, from a description of plant and animal communities to an analysis of ecosystems. Ecology courses became standard in university curricula. The Ecological Society of America, which was formed in 1915 with about 300 members, now has 5,000.[47]

Ecology has been labeled by one of its leading exponents, Paul B. Sears, "the subversive science." By this, he infers that, if taken seriously, it could "endanger the assumptions and practices accepted by modern societies, whatever their doctrinal commitments."[48]

One of the new breed of ecologists, Rachel Carson, played a pivotal part in the evolution of the modern-day environmental movement. With her early books, such as *The Sea Around Us* (1951), Miss Carson achieved fame for her understanding of nature and for the simplicity and beauty of her writing. But when she became aware of the effects on fish and wildlife of DDT and a growing list of chlorinated hydrocarbons, she found herself propelled out of the field of objective ecology into the role of political activist. In her best-seller, *Silent Spring* (1962), she compiled case studies that served to warn of the dangers that could come from too much tampering with the environment. She showed how after a lake had been sprayed with DDT, the insecticide worked its way up the food chain from plankton through fish to the birds in ever increasing concentrations until it proved fatal to the birds. And she warned that man was next in the food chain, although there was not yet evidence of the impact on man.[49]

The Popular Movement Begins

Silent Spring was significant among the accumulating factors which by the 1960s were beginning to make many Americans conscious that the old saying—"What you don't know can't hurt you"—might not be true after all. Rational people began to think about unknown and unforeseen consequences and side effects of new technological, scientific, or medical discoveries, when in the past we would have accepted the benefits of these discoveries without question.

People were also becoming aware that their environment was changing. The citizens of Los Angeles suffered increasing smog. Cleveland residents finally realized Lake Erie was in danger of "dying." Unmanaged sprawl began to spoil the advantages of suburban living. City dwellers became increasingly unhappy over crowded, noisy, polluted conditions and resented newcomers who added to the congestion of already crowded cities. The environment of the inner city worsened in a multitude of ways.

With increasingly widespread concern over the environment, interests in conservation and preservation converged, hundreds of citizen organizations were formed, new issues developed and new leaders came to the front. David Brower, executive director of the Sierra Club from 1952 to 1969, following in the footsteps of Thoreau and Muir, advocated wilderness and the rights of wild creatures, and led the national fight to keep a dam from violating the Grand Canyon.

Paul Ehrlich, in his best seller *The Population Bomb* (1968), predicted starvation and other dire effects unless population growth was controlled. Garret Hardin echoed some of the Ehrlich concerns, but presented them with ethical overtones in his "Tragedy of the Commons." Hardin drew an analogy with the old English village common (pasture), which had a large but limited "carrying capacity" that determined how many cattle it could feed. If all of the villagers each increased their herds, the carrying capacity of the common would soon be exceeded, and all would starve.[50]

Barry Commoner did not blame the environmental crisis on population growth, but warned of ecological dangers from nuclear power development, of the stresses placed on the ecological system by modern technology, and of problems associated with excessive growth. René Dubos, Ralph Nader, Lewis Mumford and many others also played major roles in alerting the public to environmental issues.

Governmental Actions

Congress responded to the increasing environmental concern and passed a federal Water Pollution Control Act in 1965, with amendments in 1970 and 1972 greatly expanding federal authority for water quality; a comprehensive Air Quality Act in 1967, with strong amendments in 1970; and solid waste disposal and resource recovery acts in 1965 and 1970. The executive branch under the Lyndon B. Johnson administration called a White House Conference on Natural Beauty. A large part of the California redwoods were set aside in a new national park, and other new national parks and historical areas were declared. A Wilderness Act was passed in 1964, making possible protection of millions of acres against mining, logging, hunting, and roads.

In 1969, a Citizens Crusade for Clean Water brought together the widest grouping of diverse organizations ever united in an environmental battle. Conservation, civic, labor, city, county and state government, consumer, church and women's organizations got together to lobby for increasing federal funds for waste water treatment plants. Due to this effective citizen lobby the appropriation was increased almost fourfold, from $217 million to $800 million.

And in late 1969, Congress passed the National Environmental Policy Act, which required federal agencies to write environmental impact statements on their major decisions affecting the environment. The act also established a Council on Environmental Quality to advise the president on environmental affairs and to coordinate environmental policy matters.

Key Events

The environmental movement as we know it today was not triggered by any one catastrophe or occurrence. But several key events had served to focus attention on environmental problems. The 1969 oil spill off Santa Barbara had an immeasurable impact. Through television, people all over the nation watched an environmental disaster as it happened. It convinced many people that they must take actions to protect their own communities from environmental harm.

The view of the earth from an American spacecraft orbiting the moon in 1969, gave all of us a perspective of our earth never before available. As astronaut Frank Borman wrote, ". . . the destinies of all who lived on it must inevitably be interwoven and joined. We are one hunk of ground, water, air, clouds, floating around in space. From out there it really is one world."

Another key event in the growing strength of the environmental movement was the Earth Day and Earth Week activities of April 1970. Although organized by students, the happenings attracted an estimated twenty million people of all ages across the nation and served as an introduction and educational stimulus for many who had never before heard of ecology and had never seen the relationship between their own activities, or those of their employers, and the environmental issues. Many discovered that ecology was not just for the tuned-in, turned-on, dropped-out ecofreaks, but was related to everyone's life and lifestyle. They began to see the relevance of comic-strip character Pogo's pollution-inspired quip: "We have met the enemy and he is us."

The Mood of the Seventies

A "new mood" was documented in the Rockefeller Brothers study, *The Use of Land*, in 1973. It revealed that citizens throughout the country were challenging traditional assumptions about the desirability of urban development because they have seen the disadvantages that unplanned growth has brought to their quality of life.[51] The Club of Rome study, *Limits to Growth*, attracted widespread attention to the stress that exponential growth of population, resource use, and pollution would place on limited natural resources. Those who tried to ignore the "limits" issue were rudely awakened when the energy crisis of 1973-74 hit young and old, rich and poor, urban and rural citizens alike. During the crisis, a number of people began to consider whether their lifestyle needed to be quite so consumption-oriented. Some found satisfaction in walking or bicycling instead of driving, in learning to get along with a thermostat turned down a few degrees, realizing that they were playing a part in solving the crisis. Just when this new ethic was beginning to take hold, however, the Arab oil embargo was lifted and the Nixon Administration declared the crisis to be ended, when it actually had only been postponed.

The pundits had looked at the temporary drop of environmental priorities in the public opinion polls after Earth Day and predicted that the environment was just a fad. Some of these same pundits are now beginning to admit that these issues will continue as long as people seek a better quality of life. Concern for the environment has been strengthened with the broadening of the issues. The numbers of those who have sought conservation and preservation have been greatly enlarged by the antipollution fighters, those interested in addressing population, food and energy problems and those seeking simpler lifestyles. For all of these reasons, concern for the environment appears now to be assured of a permanent place among citizen priorities. A 1975 public opinion poll by the Opinion Research Corporation of Princeton, New Jersey, revealed that 60 percent of the people now believe it is more important to pay the costs involved in protecting the environment than to keep prices and taxes down and run the risk of more pollution.[52] And 86 percent of the people agree that "we are paying now for the pollution caused in the past," while nine out of ten people surveyed say they believe that if we don't start cleaning up the environment now, it will cost us more money in the long run.[53]

With our increased education and rising expectations has come the conviction that we can improve our environment, and that we must do so.

Part III. Environmental Choices

The more we understand the interrelatedness of all things and the impact of our actions on our neighbors and on natural systems, the greater will be the challenge to base these choices on an environmental ethic. The influence of an environmental ethic, if it continues and grows, will bring to the surface many new issues that will confront decisionmakers at all levels with difficult choices.

Awareness of an environmental ethic appears to pit responsibility for nature and society and regard for the future on the one hand, against economic self-interest and the short-term view on the other. Many factors other than the environment enter the scene. It is the purpose of this chapter to highlight some of the issues directly connected with an environmental ethic and the critical choices they pose for us all.

We cannot rely upon the government to solve all of our environmental problems. Our wasteful habits cannot be regulated individually by the government. Yet, cumulatively, they create huge demands on our scarce resources. Nor can government exert control on so vast an area as all private investment and its diverse effects on the environment. However, it is one's decisions as an individual—at home and at work, as citizen, worker, professional, or corporate or public official—which, taken together, determine the hopes and quality of life for everyone. In all walks of life, we are presented with ethical choices as we make decisions about what will or won't be done, how it will be accomplished, and where.

Choices Illustrated

Let us examine some of these environmentally ethical choices:

You are president of a bank in a small town. A resident applies for a loan to construct a laundromat in an outlying area where the prospects of financial success are good, but where there is no sewer system. The law in your state does not require an environmental permit for a small business like this. Yet, it is possible that the detergents from the laundromat might pollute a nearby stream and affect the environment of the entire community. As a banker, do you have the responsibility to the applicant to weigh your decision only on his financial credit and ability to pay back the loan, and to the bank, to increase business? Or do you have a responsibility to the community not to make the loan? Or do you put restrictions on the loan requiring the business operator to construct a disposal system that will not pollute?

You are a receptionist in a beauty parlor and ordinarily drive your car to work. The Environmental Protection Agency says that if everybody would carpool or use the bus it would help your city meet the air pollution standards it is now violating. But to do so, you would have to walk three blocks from the bus going home. To carpool would inconvenience you. Does your responsibility to help eliminate air pollution override your own convenience? And why should you do it until everybody else does or a law is passed eliminating your parking place?

Your are an architect. A client comes to you with a plan for a shopping center to be built on a tidal marshland which he has purchased. This area is an important part of the ecosystem and future generations will depend on it to support part of the food chain, as well as on its esthetic and recreational potential. You explain to your client the environmental harm that will be done and suggest an alternate site. But the developer rejects it as too costly and insists on the wetland site. If you don't accept the job, he will get another architect to do it. Should you accept, or turn it down?

Your are a citizen in the community where the builder has requested a zoning variance for the above-mentioned project. The zoning board has called a public hearing. You believe that the development would not be in the community's long-term interest. But you feel that influential people have already gotten to the zoning board, and your voice wouldn't make any difference. You are tired after a hard day's work, and it is a rainy, cold night. Should you go to the hearing and protest the zoning variance? Or should you stay home and mind your own business?

You head a large insurance company. A representative of a national conservation organization requests a loan to purchase a swamp and hold it until the federal government can buy it for a national wildlife refuge. You cannot be absolutely certain Congress will approve the repurchase. In addition, the conservation organization asks for a rate of interest below the market, appealing to the social responsibility of your company to make the loan in the interests of the common good. You personally feel this would be in the public interest and would fall within the social responsibility of the company. But there is some risk. And you would not be getting the highest possible return on the company's money. Should you give the loan?

You are a member of the president's cabinet. Another agency has already given a permit for construction of a major amusement area within a national forest and surrounded by wilderness. But to use the area, the company would have to obtain right-of-way access through a national park, which is in your jurisdiction. Your advisors say that the road through the park would be of minor environmental harm to the park. But the National Park Service has a policy of not allowing any more roads through national parks. And the presence of thousands of people and many cars would violate the wilderness atmosphere of the national park. Should you grant the permit, or oppose it and try to stop the development?

You are chairman of the board of a major international company concerned with mining and processing natural resources. A large new deposit of ore has been found, and one of your divisions is planning to mine it. Officials at the mine have formed a committee with leading environmentalists and are seeking ways to construct the mine with the least environmental harm. This will add to the cost and may delay opening the mine. And the environmentalists might find out so much about the company's plans that they could go to court and seek to stop development. Should you stop this cooperative process because of the potential added cost and other factors which might be held against you at the next stockholders annual meeting? Or do you approve the plan as a responsible way of doing business?

Some of the above situations are hypothetical. Several of them are real choices now being made or up for decision. How individuals make these and other decisions affecting the quality of the environment now and for the future depends on two basic ingredients: the information available, and the ethics or value judgments brought to play on the choices available. The first ingredient goes hand in hand with the second: to be relevant, the information must be available in a manner which shows the interrelationships of man and nature, how one action affects another, and what the cumulative, secondary or future impacts of the decision are likely to be.

In the corporate realm a number of companies are already including environmental responsibility in their decision-making on one basis or another.

Study of Company Policies

A 1974 report by The Conference Board revealed that 86 percent of company officials surveyed considered environmental matters to be among their company's social responsibilities. Only 3 percent said that legal or community pressures were the sole consideration for their environmental program. The survey, which included 516 business corporations and utilities, also revealed that in 88 percent of the companies, environmental policy decisions are made at the level of vice president or higher. In half the companies, it was the president or chairman of the board who made the environmental policy decisions.

However, fewer than 40 percent of the companies made these decisions on the basis of any formal statement of environmental policy. Only 25 percent reported they had distinct environmental programs as part of the corporate social responsibility program. And the return of 300 of the 516 questionnaires with little or no detailed information implied that these companies either felt they had no real pollution or environmental problems or that they regarded their environmental affairs as of minimal importance.[54]

My own investigations revealed few companies having meaningful written statements of environmental policy. And even more scarce was a company with a written environmental policy that was taking special measures to implement the policy. I did find, however, a number of ways in which an environmental ethic is—or is not—being applied by business to current problems. The following case studies are presented to illustrate the character of the problems being encountered and the range of attitudes with which environmental decisions are being made.

Case Study I. AMAX. At one end of the spectrum is a case in which a company on its own, without any official or citizen protest in sight, voluntarily took costly, environmentally sound actions that promised no immediate payoff other than possible corporate public relations benefits. The setting is a new molybdenum mine in Colorado to be developed by AMAX Inc. Formerly named the American Metals Climax Company, AMAX was considered by many environmentalists to be one of the despoilers.

In the mid-1960s, a large molybdenum deposit was discovered on the other side of the Rockies, on Red Mountain, within the boundary of a scenic national forest and alongside a major transcontinental highway, an hour's drive from Denver. Because it was not a potential wilderness area, AMAX had the legal right to develop the mine within the national forest, and they traded other land they owned to the Forest Service in order to buy the parcel they would use for the mine.

In February 1967, an AMAX lawyer, Stanley Dempsey, had a chance meeting in Denver one evening with Roger Hansen, then executive director of the Colorado Open Space Coordinating Council, a consortium of regional environmental groups. Dempsey, a mountain climber and outdoor enthusiast, had been investigating what might be done in the way of environmental protection for the new mine. It would take at least seven years to develop, and Dempsey proposed to Hansen that the company and some environmentalists get together to overcome the environmental objections before they occurred. Although both realized the idea might not work, they felt it was well worth a try. First Dempsey had to sell AMAX on the concept of working out the development plans allowing this public participation. And Hansen had to convince the environmental groups that it wouldn't be a sell-out or a compromise of their principles.

They formed an ad hoc committee of five environmentalists and four AMAX representatives. Four recognized experts were among the environmentalists Hansen brought in to help: Dr. Beatrice Willard, director of the Thorne Ecological Institute (and now a member of the President's Council on Environmental Quality); Dr. E.R. Weiner, associate professor of chemistry at the University of Denver; Robert Venuti, metallurgist with the Denver Research Institute of the University of Denver; and William Mounsey, a mountain guide and wilderness advocate.

AMAX engineers saw as a challenge finding a way to design a mine that would do minimum harm to the environment, yet keep construction and operation costs within reason.

A major difficulty confronted the company over what to do about the tailings, the sandy waste left after processing the ore. Only about six *pounds* of product (molybdenum disulfide) is present per *ton* of rock. AMAX expects to process some 300 million tons of rock, 299.1 million tons of which will end up as tailings.

A milling and disposal site had to be found where the vast waste piles would have low visibility and where water and air discharges could be controlled and their polluting impact mitigated. The environmentalists assisted by visiting potential sites and making recommendations. After considering some thirty sites, the committee agreed unanimously that the Williams Fork Valley was the place where the least environmental damage would result. But the site was fourteen miles from the mine, on the *other side* of the Continental Divide. The AMAX engineers' solution was to tunnel 9.5 miles under the 12,000 foot high Continental Divide. AMAX officials accepted the plan even though it might force a delay in opening the mine, and the tunnel was estimated to cost at least $40 million. A disposal site elsewhere might initially have been less expensive. But the costs were not debated. Management accepted that it had to be done in an environmentally acceptable manner.

With the site selected, an inventory of wildlife and plant and aquatic ecology was made to provide baseline data for a continuous monitoring system. Thus the effects of the operations on the land can be determined when the mine goes into operation in 1977.

The milling site was only one part of the environmental planning. Among others:

1. The Public Service Company of Colorado, which supplies power to the site, was persuaded to work according to a plan in which trees were removed selectively by horse teams, and poles were brought in by helicopter, avoiding the need of cutting wide, straight swaths along the mountainside, as is done for most power lines. Instead of using prominently visible aluminum power poles, the Public Service Company provided wood poles which were painted various colors to blend with the vegetation.

2. The area to be cleared for the mine itself was kept to a minimum. Revegetation and tree relocation was started wherever possible. At one time

during early construction, a foreman suggested moving the road ten feet in order to save six pine trees—and it was moved.

3. AMAX opened up for public recreation the large area of private land it had acquired. When hunters began disturbing the area with recreation vehicles, AMAX barred all motor vehicles, but left the land open to the public.

4. A complex piping system was installed to route sparkling Clear Creek underneath the buildings and roads at the mine site to keep the creek from being polluted.

5. The warm water pumped from the mine is treated, cooled and run through settling ponds before being released into Clear Creek.

6. The milling and tailing site is being located so that rain and snow run-off will be diverted or caught and recycled within the mill-tailing system, rather than possibly carrying pollutants to the Williams Fork of the Colorado River.

7. Employees working on construction have become imbued with environmental consciousness to the extent that they pride themselves on maintaining the cleanliness of the construction area. In a recent tour of the site, I saw not a single candy wrapper, can or discarded lunch bag.

Stanley Dempsey feels that the environmental planning process for the new mine, which was officially labeled, "An Experiment in Ecology," was well worth the additional time and money it required. Dempsey says:

If the mining engineers and ecologists, no matter how avidly they feel, can learn to respect each other's judgment and listen to one another, then we're going to come out with decisions that make some sense. The more openly we do it, the more objective we can become and the better the decisions will be. Mining is legitimate, and necessary. But so are environmental activities.

I thought that working with ecologists might make our engineers and our management more sensitive to sound environmental interests. But I also felt that tne environmentalists, by working with our people, would listen to the arguments and agree that some of their own ideas were not practical. I thought it would be a real start of a new generation of mining activity with environmental concern.

While this millenium has not yet been reached, the success of the Experiment in Ecology has had a beneficial side effect at AMAX. Back in 1967, when the experiment started, AMAX not only lacked a structure to deal with environmental problems, but had no means of crossing divisional lines to work out common problems. In 1970, AMAX board chairman, Ian MacGregor, encouraged by Dempsey's environmental planning process, called fifty representatives from the company's operating divisions to Denver for a discussion of environmental activities and to tell what their divisions were doing in that area. Chairman MacGregor attended all the meetings at the two-and-a-half day conference. At the end, he suggested it was time that an environmental structure be formalized. An AMAX Environmental Planning and Protection Committee was formed, with eighteen people representing base metals, lead and zinc mining, milling, molybdenum and special metals, fuels and chemicals, aluminum, and financial and corporate people from headquarters. Various task forces were set up and policies reviewed.

The committee has held a number of its meetings on site at plants. At these meetings, the host division discusses its own environmental problems and tells or shows what it is doing about them. Dempsey said:

We got a dialogue going within the company. For instance, there were differences of opinion on problems such as occupational health and safety for employees within a plant versus external environmental considerations. The safety people wanted to blow all of the gas out of a certain plant to protect the workers. But the environmental engineer had to prevent the gas from going up the stack and breaking the air pollution laws. We were able to break down the communication barriers and help thrash this problem out.

In November 1973, a second special, company-wide environmental meeting was held at Tucson, Arizona, with 100 people attending, including board chairman Ian MacGregor. Out of the meeting came the formation of a full corporate department known as the Environmental Services Group. The Denver-based operation now has a staff of sixteen, including a field ecologist, a wildlife biologist, two environmental control engineers, a mining engineer and a sanitation engineer, an attorney, two financial analysts, and a geographer. It is headed by Dempsey. All divisions that are planning new developments must now discuss their projects with the Environmental Services Group, and all capital appropriation requests related to environment controls must now pass through the Environmental Services Group for review.

The day I visited Dempsey he had just been talking with an official from the coal mining division about what kind of reclamation should be done on a coal strip mine being planned. He said,

There's a lot of feeling in the mining industry that if you can get corn to grow on mined land, that's reclamation. We feel that it is not enough. We should also be concerned about repairing the ecosystem and restoring wildlife habitats. And if we do decide to grow corn on the reclaimed land, we don't need to plow right up to the edge of the stream. Maybe we could leave a little cover for the wildlife. In a food-short world, agriculture probably should be given preference, but diversity of the land will eventually be proven to be important in developing both wildlife and cash crops.

Board Chairman MacGregor says that initial costs are obviously greater when you plan and carry out a project in an environmentally correct way. MacGregor said,

We realize that these things are the costs of doing business today. It's just good business to solve the environmental problems to the best of your ability before you start. Business is supposed to look at the quality of life for the people. My point of view is that we should look at the *real* bottom line—that is, we need that molybdenum in the 1980s and if we don't produce molybdenum in a way that is consistent with the environment, then we're not in business. And I mean the total environment, including the economic, the political and the public understanding of what's good and what's bad. A lot of people will take the view that the way to solve the problem of opposition from environmentalists is to do it your way and take your baseball bat in the other hand and beat away the people who want to stop you. That belongs in another age.

I believe that in our particular business we've got to establish our own reputation by doing the things that we see should be done. And even if we can't convince all the population, we can convince people in our own immediate surroundings that we're doing things reasonably right, and that includes building in responsibility for the environment.

Despite the good results at the Henderson mine, AMAX's environmental efforts are not always successful, and several present operations being planned by the company are under attack by environmentalists for one reason or another. Dempsey feels the Experiment in Ecology at the Henderson mine cannot necessarily be repeated in all situations. But he believes the general lessons learned from it can be applied in other situations. He says

The first thing is that people in the mining business have to admit that any sizable operation is going to cause change in the area—it can't be the same as it was before. Next, any industry should try to identify groups that can assist in the design of the property to minimize this environmental impact. Third, is the need for a natural resources inventory to use as a measure on which to base potential environmental impact. The inventory should be started at the earliest possible moment. The company should build redundancy into its planning—how will we respond if things don't work out as they have been planned? And finally, there is a need for continuously generating and sharing information.

Case Study II. Reserve Mining. Another case study presents the issue of environmental responsibility under quite different circumstances.

Who should have the burden of proof—government or industry—when a product or a process of industry is suspected of having side effects harmful to human health, yet conclusive, clear evidence is not available one way or the other? This issue has come out in the environmental problems of the Reserve Mining Company of Silver Bay, Minnesota.

Reserve Mining, a wholly-owned subsidiary of Republic Steel Corporation and Armco Steel Corporation, has been dumping waste tailing from its taconite processing into Lake Superior since the plant opened in 1955. It received permits in 1947, after the state held extended hearings.

The company mines taconite ore in Minnesota's Mesabi Range, and then transports it by rail fifty-five miles to the processing plant built on the shore of Lake Superior, sixty miles north of Duluth, at the mining town of Silver Bay. Other companies also mine taconite in the Mesabi Range, but do their processing at the site, and run their tailing through a closed recirculating system of ponds.

Federal investigations and legal skirmishes had been going on since 1969. After a series of enforcement conferences between the federal government and a number of Lake Superior polluters, all except Reserve agreed on abatement schedules to curb their pollution. When no agreements could be reached with Reserve, the federal Environmental Protection Agency, the state of Minnesota, and some environmental organizations went to federal court in 1973 alleging violation of federal and state water and air pollution laws and violations of laws against dumping of wastes.

The public health issue had become a national interest matter in late 1972, when researchers identified particles of the tailings dumped into the lake by Reserve as being potentially harmful. Samples of these fibers have since been found in the drinking water at Duluth and other places around the lake. Expert medical testimony at the Federal District Court trial early in 1974, predicted that these elements could possibly cause cancer if swallowed in significant amounts over a period of years, but it might take another ten to twenty years before the illness would develop. And the Justice Department's pleading said that the Reserve tailings contained thirty-five chemical materials including arsenic, beryllium, selenium and thallium—all toxic materials.

On April 20, 1974, Federal District Judge Miles W. Lord ordered the plant to cease its discharges to the air and water, thus closing down the plant. However, a three-judge Circuit Court of Appeals panel stayed the order and the plant was reopened, after being closed thirty-two hours.

After continued litigation, the full Eighth Circuit Court of Appeals ruled that Reserve Mining must within a reasonable time stop discharging fibers into the air and into Lake Superior from the Silver Bay plant, but sent the case back to District Court to determine a reasonable period of time for compliance. "The United States and other plaintiffs have established that Reserve's discharges into the air and water give rise to a potential threat to the public health," the court said. But it ruled that no harm to the public health has been shown to have occurred to this date, and the danger to health is not imminent. The air pollution problem was ruled most dangerous, and the court required Reserve to "take reasonable immediate steps" to reduce its air emissions with a minimum disruption of the labor force.

Hearings have been held in Minnesota to determine the feasibility of the alternate site now suggested by Reserve. And the company has agreed to reduce the air discharges.

I went to Minnesota and looked into the situation and talked with representatives of both sides. A company official showed me through the plant, and took me by boat out to see the dumping in the lake. I saw close up the two outlets where 67,000 tons of ground rock tailings flow each day into Lake Superior, the largest fresh water lake in the world, and known for its purity. Most of the tailings go into the deep trough of the lake, the company official said, although some of the coarser particles remain to build up a delta outside the plant. The green water that many observers had frequently seen in the lake in recent years was not caused by Reserve Mining, he said, but was due to unexplained causes. It was a rare occurrence in the Silver Bay area, he added. The company had received permits in 1947, which are still valid, he claimed. Reserve had even offered to build a pipe to extend the dumping into deeper parts of the lake, but this was refused by Minnesota and the federal government.

Dr. Arnold Brown, chairman of the Department of Pathology and Anatomy of the Mayo Clinic, was appointed by the District Court as its chief impartial expert witness for the trial. Dr. Brown testified that he saw no evidence of an increased incidence of cancer at present in communities near the plant that could be attributed to the presence of asbestos fibers in air or water. Dr. Brown also testified that the scientific evidence was not complete enough to draw a conclusion one way or the other concerning the problem of a future public health hazard from the water.

Reserve had offered during the trial to prepare a land dumping site near the plant, at a cost of $185 million, but the state rejected the plan because it was to be built on prime recreation land. Reserve, I was told, has now surveyed another land site in the Lax Lake basin near the plant to which they are prepared to move the tailing disposal, if the state will give them a permit. It would be financially impossible, a company official said, to move the whole plant to the Mesabi range (cost of $669 million) where the ore is produced. And they could not send the tailing sludge back to the ore site because it would freeze in the sub-zero winter conditions. The company official added that if Reserve was not now allowed to build the dumping site in the Lax Lake basin, and was denied permission to dump in Lake Superior, the company would be forced to go out of business, throwing 3,000 employees out of work at Silver Bay and at Babbitt, where the ore is mined. And it would force the nation to lose ten percent of its supply of iron ore, which would have to be imported from foreign countries. Under these circumstances, the official said, it was not fair to ask the company to accept responsibility or to apply environmentally ethical considerations, inasmuch as the government had not proved there was any health danger.

From Grant J. Merritt, then executive director of the Minnesota Pollution Control Agency, from lawyers in the case, and from citizens in neighboring Beaver Bay, I obtained a different picture of the Reserve case. The Appellate Court, even while overruling the injunction on closing the plant, said that the original 1947 permits to allow Reserve to dump its wastes into Lake Superior was a "monumental environmental mistake." Reserve, the state contended, was now violating virtually all the conditions of those permits, including one which forbade the discharge should it ever threaten public drinking water supplies. At the trial, expert witness Dr. Irving J. Selikoff, director of the environmental sciences laboratory at the Mount Sinai School of Medicine, New York, said that although no positive evidence of carcinogenic effects from the asbestos discharge could be proved now, no type of asbestos can be regarded as free from hazard. He compared the continuing pollution of Lake Superior with "asbestiform" fibers to a game of Russian roulette. "I don't know where the bullet is located," he testified, "But if we are wrong, then the consequences of that error are disastrous. Moreover . . . while we play the game, others will pay the penalty."

Merritt said the air pollution potential is even worse than the water problems. Some air samples revealed up to 11 million asbestos fibers per cubic meter (and up to 140 million if a sample taken at the top of one of the plant's smokestacks is included).

The trial revealed that Reserve has been making large profits, and Merritt said the company should have started finding an alternate solution years ago, when the health hazards first came up.

The two sites Reserve has picked for land disposal are both prime recreation land and should not be used for dumping of tailings, Merritt said. The first site, close to Lake Superior, also would have caused a hazard to the lake should the retaining dam break. And the second proposed site would have ruined a spectacularly scenic lake and heavily-wooded area. The Federal District Court found that "it is indisputable that Reserve's discharge into the water of Lake Superior is in violation" of federal law, the discharge into the air and water create "a common law nuisance" that violates both federal common law and the applicable state laws of nuisance, and the discharges substantially endanger the health of those exposed to it in Minnesota, Wisconsin, and Michigan.

I asked Merritt about the conscious decisions of the workers at the plant, who, if given the choice, apparently would continue the present exposure risks in order to continue their jobs. Do they have an ethical right to make this choice? Merritt pointed to Judge Lord's decision which said:

If in fact the people of Silver Bay were the only ones exposed to the health risk there might be some weight to be given their conscious choice to take the associated risk involved to continue at their jobs. Even then, however, the Court would have to take a broader view of the matter. In the first place, the Court would be concerned with those who were unable to make a real choice, particularly the children who must abide by their parents. Secondly, this Court would have to answer the question, 'can this Court permit a commercial industry to require its work force to make such a choice that endangers their lives and the lives of their families, when in fact the commercial industry has the economic and technological means to eliminate any real health risk?' Consistent with governmental regulation of industrial safety and health conditions, the obvious answer is NO. In that Reserve's discharge largely endangers the lives of thousands in other communities unrelated to the activity of the company it becomes even more clear that the discharge must stop.

Merritt says that even though Reserve has agreed to end its dumping, the key question is *when!* "The question remains and it is a crucial question involving public health implications of the gravest magnitude, as to *when* the dumping will cease."

Other Burden of Proof Cases. The Reserve Mining case is one of a number which has drawn public attention to the issue of where the responsibility lies when an action carries the potential of unknown future side effects that may harm health or seriously damage land or an ecosystem. The public has already been alerted to the dangers of long-term and sometimes delayed side effects, as in the widely publicized thalidomide and DDT issues. A few years later the Supersonic Transport (SST) drew the spotlight, with a major argument against the plane being its possibly harmful effects on the upper atmosphere. Leading scientists theorized that a fleet of 500 SSTs might upset the ozone layer in the stratosphere (from about ten to thirty miles above the earth), reducing the ozone at a faster rate than it is naturally replaced and thereby letting potentially hazardous ultraviolet radiation through to the earth. The scientists who suggested this could not prove their theory; government scientists could not prove the theory false. The government said, let's go ahead and continue research. By the time we have 500 planes in the sky we should know if they will be harmful. The environmentalists said: "Why the rush? Just because the technology is available, does that mean we have to do it? Why not wait to build the planes until we do the research and find out if there are harmful effects?"

Congress voted down the SST on economic grounds, because other domestic needs had greater priority for funds. Thus the atmospheric effects did not become the chief issue.

A recent example of unforeseen and as yet unproved danger is related to impacts from use of certain fluorocarbons. The concern has surfaced with reports of scientists, including a National Academy of Science study, indicating that fluorocarbon gases emitted from common aerosol spray cans used for hair dressings, paints, insecticides and automotive products, or gases from refrigeration equipment, may be causing a depletion of the ozone layer. This could lead to a rise in skin cancer, damage plants and phytoplantkton, and possibly affect the weather in an adverse manner. The theory is that the gases, such as Freon, used as propellants and released in the use of the products, break down when exposed to the ultraviolet rays in the stratosphere.

The Academy report suggested that the amount of propellant currently in the atmosphere could reduce the ozone layer by 1 percent, causing a 1 percent rise in skin cancer. But because of year-to-year fluctuations that occur naturally in the ozone layer, the effect might not become certain until the depletion rate rose to 10 percent—and that could increase the skin cancer incidence by 10 percent.

Industry responded that such effects had not been proved. "All we have are assumptions," said Dr. Raymond L. McCarthy, technical director of the Freon Products Division of E.I. Du Pont de Nemours & Co. "Without experimental evidence, it would be an injustice if a few claims—which even the critics agree are hypotheses—were to be the basis of regulatory or consumer reaction." He said that research would be undertaken immediately by fluorocarbon makers in the United States and abroad to simulate the chemical reactions affecting the survival of ozone in the lower stratosphere.[55]

Two weeks after release of the first report, the Natural Resources Defense Council petitioned the federal government's Consumer Product Safety Commission to outlaw the use of fluorocarbons in aerosol spray cans. On July 31, 1975, the states of Oregon, New York, and Michigan joined NRDC in its petition.[56] The states' action came in the wake of the release of a five-month study by a federal interagency task force that concluded "that fluorocarbon releases to the environment are legitimate cause for concern." The study recommended "unless new scientific evidence is found to remove the cause for concern" that fluorocarbons used as aerosol propellants be banned by January 1978.[57]

Again the leading flurocarbon aerosol industry went on record in "strong disagreement" with the task force findings, labeling the study as premature.[58]

The issue is thus whether government or industry accepts responsibility for potential harm to public health. Should the aerosol manufacturers withdraw their cans from the market, absorb whatever financial loss is necessary, and use substitute dispensers until scientific evidence is clear one way or the other? Or should they wait and see if the government moves to withdraw the cans? Should the government wait until research has been done before it takes action? If the government takes action, should the companies appeal and delay the decision?

Responsibility to Stockholders. Another type of environmental decision facing corporate leaders is: How rigidly must they abide by the doctrine of responsibility to shareholders and employees to assure that the company makes as large a profit as possible? The vice president of one of the nation's largest insurance companies, for instance, took the position that his company could not possibly develop or accept any code of environmental ethics or allow purely environmental concerns to enter into decisions—unless they were related directly to profit-making. He said his sole responsibility was to enlarge profits in the interests of the policy holders, investors in the company, and employees.

But the head of the real estate division of one of that company's regional offices, which lends millions of dollars each year to development projects, had a more moderate outlook. He admitted to me that he personally felt that the company should consider environmental factors in the loan process as a social responsibility to the communities affected by the developments on which money was loaned. He said he felt the company would refuse to give loans on projects where the developer might run into trouble getting environmental pollution permits, but that there was no actual written policy.

Case Study III. Aetna. Another insurance company, Aetna Life & Casualty, does have a stated corporate social responsibility policy. It includes provisions such as denying any liability protection to businesses that knowingly and wantonly pollute the environment. Aetna also uses its own laboratory analysis to detect products potentially dangerous to consumers, in companies to be insured. Its board chairman, John H. Filer, is personally committed to environmental protection and natural resource preservation. Filer is also seeking ways of making Aetna's investment policy more responsive to social and environmental concerns. An example of this involves a request from The Nature Conservancy, a nonprofit conservation organization which has preserved thousands of acres of ecologically vital private land. One method the Conservancy uses is to quickly purchase lands when they become available, and hold them until a federal, state or local body can obtain funds to obtain the lands.

The Conservancy needed a large loan to purchase 14,000 acres of the Great Dismal Swamp in Virginia, an area which the federal Fish and Wildlife Service hoped to obtain for a wildlife refuge, but which had not been authorized by Congress. Ordinarily, the Conservancy would draw on a line of credit at a bank. But when the land-purchase opportunity came up, the interest rate was 12 percent, too high for the organization to absorb. (The Conservancy would buy the land below the assessed valuation and recoup its costs and interest when the federal government purchased it later at the assessed valuation price.)

The Conservancy president, Patrick Noonan, approached Aetna Board Chairman Filer, whom he had met previously when Filer chaired a local conservation meeting in Connecticut, and requested a loan below the market.

"I pointed out," says Noonan, "that Aetna loaned a lot of money for construction and development—so they should make special efforts to loan money for conservation. And I said that the company would also be subsidizing security for other loans on housing and industry in the area because preservation of the land would enhance the quality of life for the people in the area."

Filer and Aetna's vice president for Corporate Social Responsibility, Edwin B. Knauft, considered the request. "We wouldn't ordinarily make a loan on a swamp," Knauft says. "And there was some risk that Congress would not authorize the refuge or appropriate the money, and we might end up holding a swamp that we would then have to sell to a lumber company."

But Aetna discovered that the Nature Conservancy had a record of no failures in eighty lending transactions. And an assistant secretary of the interior verified that the area, Great Dismal Swamp, was a top priority for federal acquisition. Aetna agreed not only to give the loan, but also to do so on terms several percentage points below the going interest rate.

"Normally a situation like this would have required a higher rate of interest than the market because of the risk involved," said Knauft. "But we feel that conservation is a part of our social responsibility, and one of the things we can do as a large company is to lead the way for other companies."

Aetna Chairman Filer says the company is proud to be part of an investment opportunity "that offers as its return the preservation of the last true wilderness on the mid-Atlantic seaboard. These tracts of land are of such significance and special value that the Great Dismal Swamp fully warrants our support and involvement. Aetna's loan of $1.7 million to the Conservancy reflects our position that private profit does indeed benefit the public good."

Other Land Saving Cases. Two other insurance companies, Northwestern National Life Insurance Company of Minneapolis and Equitable Life Assurance Society of the United States, have also loaned money to The Nature Conservancy for land preservation purposes at "favorable" rates below the prime. Equitable financed the $1.3 million purchase by the Conservancy of a 3,855-acre salt marsh north of Atlantic City, New Jersey, in the path of the Atlantic Flyway bird migratory route.[59] Equitable also carried a major portion of the financing for the $2 million purchase of 1,708 acres of the Sandhill Crane Sanctuary in Jackson County, Mississippi, the last known colony of the Mississippi sandhill crane, which is threatened with extinction. Both of these areas are to be added to the Federal Wildlife Refuge system.[60] Northwestern helped the Conservancy in the purchase of 25 miles of lake shore and 4,500 acres north of Grand Rapids, Minn.[61] This area will be purchased after congressional approval by the U.S. Forest Service. These transactions also contained an added element of individual citizen concern for the common good because all of the owners sold the properties well below the market price.

Case Study IV. Mineral King. An area of environmental ethical choices which sometimes involves profits and always arouses dedicated preservationists is the issue of humanity's responsibility for nature.

A case that has gained national attention concerns the possibility that a major ski resort might be developed in the Mineral King Valley of California's Sierra Nevada mountains. Although mining activity took place in the valley years ago, it had few signs of civilization by 1969. The valley lies within the Sequoia National Forest and is bordered partly by wilderness sectors of the National Forest and Sequoia National Park. But the U.S. Forest Service agreed in 1969 to lease the valley to Walt Disney Enterprises for a projected $35 million ski resort of motels, restaurants, swimming pools, parking lots, and other structures to accommodate 14,000 visitors a day. The Sierra Club sued the secretary of the interior because he had agreed to give access to the area across Sequoia National Park. A U.S. District Court granted the Sierra Club an injunction on the basis that the club had "a special interest in the conservation and sound maintenance of the national parks, game refuges, and forests of the country."[62]

The Ninth Circuit Court of Appeals reversed the lower court decision. And the Supreme Court, in a case known particularly for its dissents by Justices William O. Douglas and Harry A. Blackmun, upheld the appellate court on a 4-3 verdict (Justices Powell and Rehnquist took no part in the case). The majority opinion by Justice Potter Stewart upheld the legal point of the Court of Appeals that the Sierra Club lacked "standing" to sue. The court did not reach any other of the several environmental questions raised by the Sierra Club. The Stewart opinion did indicate, however, that individual members of the club could sue on their own if they could show that they were affected in any of their activities or pastimes by the Disney development.

Justice Blackmun dissented vigorously, claiming that as a result of the majority opinion, this area of great natural beauty "will become defaced, at least in part, and like so many other areas will cease to be 'uncluttered by the products of civilization.' "[63] He argued that the Sierra Club should have been given standing to sue. And he closed by citing the warning of John Donne:

No man is an Iland, intire of itselfe; every man is a piece of the Continent, a part of the maine; if a Clod bee washed away by the Sea, Europe is the lesse, as well as if a Promontorie were, as well as if a Mannor of they friends or of thine owne were; any man's death diminishes me, because I am involved in Mankinde; And therefore never send to know for whom the bell tolls; it tolls for thee." (Devotions XVII)[64]

Justice Douglas' dissent argued that "contemporary public concern for protecting nature's ecological equilibrium should lead to the conferral of standing upon environmental objects to sue for their own preservation."[65] Justice Douglas wrote:

In the same way that a ship or an ordinary corporation is a "person" for adjudicatory processes, so it should be as respects valleys, alpine meadows, rivers, lakes, estuaries, beaches, ridges, groves of trees, swampland, or even air that feels the destructive pressures of modern technology and modern life. The river, for example, is the living symbol of all the life it sustains or nourishes— fish, aquatic insects, water ouzels, otter, fishes, deer, elk, bear, and all other animals, including man, who are dependent on it or who enjoy it for its sight, its sound, or its life. The river as plaintiff speaks for the ecological unit of life that is part of it. Those people who have a meaningful relation to that body of water—whether it be a fisherman, a canoeist, a zoologist, or a logger—must be able to speak for the values which the river represents and which are threatened with destruction.[66]

But on a more practical level, Justice Douglas argued that the inarticulate members of the ecological group cannot speak! "But those people who have so frequented the place as to know its values and wonders will be able to speak for the entire ecological community."[67]

Although environmentalists lost the court case, other legal delays and unfavorable publicity resulted in the Disney corporation abandoning Mineral King and choosing another site for their winter resort development.

The Responsibility for Nature Issue

The issue of responsibility for Nature is extremely volatile at present, and the arguments are often more emotional than legal. At one extreme are those who take the position that nature is to serve man. This point of view argues that if man needs more electric power in Southern California, and the most economical way to get it is to place huge power dams along the Colorado River near Grand Canyon, that is the right thing to do. Under these assumptions, forests are leveled, wildlife habitat destroyed, wetlands taken over for subdivisions or agriculture. This attitude values whales only for food and products, seals and tigers only for skins, and sees wolves as enemies of mankind.

At the other extreme are some who claim that all nature, even rocks, should have legal and moral rights. Leading exponents of this theory held a conference in April 1974, at Pitzer College, California, on "The Rights of Non-Human Nature." Participants based much of their discussion on Christopher Stone's book: *Should Trees Have Standing? Toward Legal Rights for Natural Objects.* Several discussants theorized that no part of the ecosystem has any right over any other because all parts sustain every other, themselves, and the whole system. Thus, humans must be viewed only as parts of the whole.

There is a growing acceptance of a position somewhere between these extremes that can be perceived as a measure of the developing environmental ethic. Those who hold this moderate position believe in the responsibility to protect and preserve nature and wildlife, but they do not bestow on nature any absolute rights. They say, for instance: How can one seek absolute ethical and legal rights for animals which themselves do not live by ethical codes, but in most cases live by a code of survival? They also point to the theory of evolution which indicates that species have become extinct, land formations have changed drastically, apart from man's influence, yet the universe survives.

A growing part of our society feels that there are limits to the man-centered view, that we should not take the Biblical bestowal on man of dominion over all the earth as blanket permission to use nature indiscriminately. They point to Bible translations of the word "dominion" to mean "stewardship," and feel man has a responsibility to act as a steward. They feel that whales should not become extinct, that wild rivers should not all be tamed, that wilderness and wildlife habitats and places of natural beauty should be preserved whenever possible—in sum, that these things are necessary for the wholeness of an ecosystem in which man is compatible with nature.

An example of the middle-ground position of responsibility for nature can be found in the American tradition of national parks. They symbolize a nation's commitment to preserve areas, not just to serve our wants, but as setting in which we agree to accept nature on its own terms. By setting aside more than thirty million acres in national parks, with another thirty million or more scheduled to be set aside in Alaska, Americans have accepted a limitation on how they use the land. They agree that exploitation will not be allowed within a national park. After the Hetch Hetchy dam was built in Yosemite half a century ago, no other dam has been allowed in a national park. Hunting is outlawed in almost all national parks. So are logging and mining. Roads are kept at a minimum. Amenities such as tennis courts, swimming pools, golf courses are almost entirely excluded. Although the parks are to be enjoyed by people, we also give nature a large degree of privilege. And we preserve the parks for future generations to enjoy—another part of the environmental ethic.

At Everglades National Park in Florida, a few years ago, a water moccasin snake was observed alongside a nature trail, and a ranger was called. Instead of killing the snake, one of four types of poisonous reptiles in the nation, Ranger Saul Schiffman attempted to catch it alive in order to remove it to a wild part of the park. But while he was attempting to catch the snake, it bit him. He put it in a box before he went to the hospital. He survived. And the snake was released in the interior swampland.

At Yellowstone National Park, feeding of bears from the autos on the highway is now forbidden; most of the black bears no longer frequent the roadside, and visitors seldom see them. Some visitors complain. But most accept this as the rights of the animals to live a natural existence.

Yet, the ethic is not followed absolutely. When two young women were killed by grizzly bears at Glacier National Park a few years ago, the offending bears were hunted down and destroyed, even though the bears could be said to have been exercising their territorial rights and that the victims had been encroaching on those rights.

At the conference on "the Rights of Non-Human Nature," a moderating voice was raised by Garrett Hardin, author of the "Tragedy of the Commons" and "Lifeboat Ethics" essays. He could not agree with those who advocated absolute rights for nature, saying that some things cannot be legislated, and attempts to do so are merely attempts to rationalize everything. "Nature is a fiction created by the human psyche when we seek to avoid responsibility for the heart's decisions," he said. "The voice of Nature is man's voice. The rights of nature are created by man." He added that we must come to accept personal, human choices (the heart) rather than having the law tell us what is right, what has rights.

Environmental Codes of Ethics

A voluntary means of forwarding environmental responsibility is for businesses, professions, or their associations to draw up codes for practicing an environmental ethic. Such codes usually fail, however, for lack of enforcement, or because some businesses or individuals in the group will not agree to the code.

Bankers' Pollution Code. One such attempt was made in Maine four years ago when the Maine Bankers Association drew up a "Pollution Code." The code's originator, Halsey Smith, was chairman of the board of the Casco Bank and Trust Company of Portland at the time he introduced it. (He is presently director of the Center for Research and Advanced Studies at the University of Maine.) He sold the idea to his own bank as a means of expressing environmental responsibility in the community, and also as a protection against lending to developers who might default if they ran afoul of environmental hazards which stopped their projects.

Maine law required permits for developments covering 60,000 square feet or 20 acres or more.[68] But there were no laws regulating the environmental effects of smaller developments which individually or cumulatively could harm an area.

The bankers' code stated that 'pollution control and abatement must be an integral consideration in credit decisions attendant to the financing of new industries, expansion of existing industries and new and existent commercial ventures to insure that such financing shall not encourage or abet pollution of the air, land or water of the State of Maine."[69]

The code specified six points on which banking institutions and the association were to act:

1. The banking institutions are to satisfy themselves that "by virtue of the granting of such credit, no significant pollution of air, land or water will result";
2. They will cooperate fully with the Environmental Improvement Commission of the state;
3. The institutions and association will accept informal expert opinion from the state Environmental Improvement Commission in instances wherein licensing is not required, as to whether or not significant pollution of air, land or water could result from approval of the credit request;
4. The institutions and association will make every effort to offer alternative programs or techniques to avoid pollution when it is self-evident that significant pollution may result, and will stand ready to advance amounts of additional credit to effect changes necessary to eliminate pollution, assuming that the credit is within the ability of both customer and institution;
5. The institutions and association will seek to persuade customers who are presently polluting the air, land or water of Maine, of the urgency, "for the future well-being of the State, to abate their present pollutant practices," and when possible, to offer additional credit to permit abatement;
6. The institution or banking association agree to use such powers of persuasion as they may possess to persuade their counterparts in other states to adopt voluntary codes similar to this, not only for requests to finance projects in Maine, but for requests in their own states.[70]

"In this age you don't sell moral responsibility very easily," Smith says. "I got my bank to go along with the idea. But only twenty-two banks in the association—just half of its members—voted to adopt the code. As a result, it bombed."

It could have succeeded only if all the banks had adopted it, or if the association had some enforcement power. As it was, the banks that did sign said they could not abide by the code unless their competitors did so too, or they would lose business.

"I argued that they turned down loans that their competitors accepted, for other reasons, so what was wrong with doing it for environmental reasons?" Smith says.

The present director of the Maine Bankers Association, Roger Ayers, told me he did not know if the code was being followed. The implication was that the code was primarily a paper exercise. Ayers said the Association has done no follow-up on it since it was passed. But he believes it has resulted in some benefits, and that it has at least sparked an awareness of environmental problems in some bank officers.

A similar pollution code was adopted by the New Jersey Bankers Association in May 1970, although it was not submitted to member banks for approval. No enforcement provision was included, and there has been no follow-up by the association.

An International Code for Industry

In the international area, a worldwide code of guidelines for industry's responsibility toward the environment was prepared by the International Chamber of Commerce (ICC) and adopted by the Chamber's Executive Committee in June 1974. The voluntary code was presented to governments, the public and companies "for information and consideration."

The International Chamber noted that industrial operations "necessarily have a substantial though by no means exclusive influence on the quality of the environment. This influence may sometimes be negative but can also often be positive."

The policy statement carries no request for acceptance by individual nations or companies, and has no enforcement mechanism. Yet, it presents guidelines for industry's future coordination and cooperation with other elements in government and other elements of society. The guidelines adopted are necessarily broad, but they were framed to be applicable to industry in developing countries as well as in most industrialized areas. They are to apply not only to manufacturing, but equally to transport, tourism, public utilities and agriculture.

Among key parts of the code, approved by the ICC's governing body, representing forty-nine national ICC committees, was the stipulation that industry, in designing new plants and extensions to existing plants, should seek to forestall pollution by applying the most appropriate pollution abatement measures, technically proven, economically acceptable and consistent with local requirements.

The opening statement of the thirty-four principles declares: "Industry recognizes that, in the environmental context as in others, it must operate as an integral and responsible member of the community . . . to contribute to the community in an atmosphere of understanding and encouragement." The code suggests the need for better management of nonrenewable resources, taking into account the interrelationship between environmental considerations and resource availability. It also recognizes the need for land reclamation upon the completion of industrial projects.

One part of the code urges industry to develop a resource conservation program. Each company should promote in its employees, an individual sense of environmental responsibility, and for its customers, provide advice on conservation, reuse and recycling. Another section calls for industry to make every effort to minimize any adverse environmental impact of its products under reasonable conditions of usage and to ensure that this impact is assessed in the case of new products in advance of their release to the market.

Regulatory approaches, according to the code, should be based upon the establishment of environmental standards which permit technological flexibility in reaching the desired goal.

Economic Debate

Despite arguments in favor of making choices to do what is most environmentally sound, the counter factor of self-interest is always present, especially when profits and economic considerations are at stake. Economists argued vigorously over the extent of businesses' social and other responsibilities long before the environmental situation was acute. Forty years ago, two distinguished British economists, John Maynard Keynes and A.C. Pigou, debated the issue.

Lord Keynes, in the 1930s, had advocated maximizing national income through increased productivity, regardless of social costs. Pigou, on the other hand, was concerned with the equitable distribution of the national income as a contribution to a morally acceptable society. He advocated finding ways for the economic system to account for the "external disservices," which included disruptions of the natural environment.

The present-day extremes are represented by contemporary economic theorists Milton Friedman and Ezra Mishan. The Milton Friedman school sees businesses' exclusive responsibility as the maximization of profit. Mishan, on the other hand, would restrain economic self-interest by conferring the "right to amenity" on citizens, and would force business and industry, in their quest for profits, to compensate citizens for damages suffered in consequence of production.

Another school of economic and environmental thought argues for a steady state or equilibrium economy as the only environmentally sound and ecologically sustainable form of human society. Kenneth Boulding and Herman Daly are leading present-day advocates of the steady-state economy, although the need was perceived and discussed long ago by Adam Smith and John Stuart Mill. The transition to material equilibrium in a steady-state, sustainable society is being studied by many groups, including the Jay Forrester team at Massachusetts Institute of Technology, Dennis and Donella Meadows at Dartmouth, and the "Search for a Sustainable Society" Seminar at MIT under Carroll Wilson and David Dodson Gray.

A steady-state economy and sustainable society do not imply an end to all forms of growth, but simply a sharp limit upon forms of growth that damage our life-setting. Steady state may be defined as: A stable population that takes from the environment no more each year than is grown in a year, reduces to a minimum its use of raw materials that once used cannot be replaced, and reduces to a minimum all pollution and waste that must be discarded into the environment. To achieve its goals, the stock of productive capital goods is stabilized and what is produced is made to be much more durable, able to be repaired and eventually recycled.

Many economists believe that the market system can be relied upon to guide us in all the necessary steps needed to live in harmony with our environmental setting. Environmental requirements, they argue, can be built into the market price of goods and services by including in the price the "external costs" borne not by the producer but by the rest of society after the production process. Environmentalists argue that no pricing system exists or could exist for assessing all of the present and subsequent true environmental costs, including the price of restoring health to individuals and to the ecosystem, and of replenishing the earth for future generations.

"I incline to believe we have overestimated the scope of the profit motive," Aldo Leopold wrote in one of his last essays. "Is it profitable for the individual to build a beautiful home? To give his children a higher education? No, it is seldom profitable, yet we do both."[71]

The Critical Choice

Whether environmental citizenship is achieved by more adequate pricing of total costs within the market system, by broader and more inclusive measures to adjust our lifestyles and expectations to a gentler impact upon our environment, or by a transition—either abrupt or gradual—to some steady state sustainable society, clearly the choice is critical.

It may take a turning from material satisfactions to higher, to spiritual values. It may take a new sense of religion, not necessarily formal but measured in a better understanding of our relationship to the whole of creation, and an acceptance of the responsibilities for the effects of our actions not only upon ourselves and humankind, but upon our total environment.

The obvious desire for survival is a basic consideration. But what kind of environment do we want once survival is assured? And what kind of life can we want for our children—and for future generations?

The environmental ethic, like any ethic, requires of the individual a concern for the *summum bonum*, the highest or greatest good for all people, land, and wildlife. Its acceptance may be difficult in the developing nations, or among the deprived in our nation and elsewhere in the industrial world, wherever food, shelter and employment are a constant struggle. But there is no reason why most of us cannot in some measure build into our decision-making at least a concern for the environment and a willingness to consider alternative courses of action which may be more environmentally responsible.

Idealistic—perhaps. Acceptance of environmental citizenship would challenge widely-held economic assumptions and practices, especially in the business sector. Finding ways to replace narrow, short-range, bottom-line thinking with long-range, socially concerned decision-making will not be easy. Some subjugation of personal gain to the common need will be required. But it can be done, even though along the way compromises will be required from the absolutists on both sides.

Notes

Part I. The Need for an Environmental Ethic

1. Economic Research Service, "Major Uses of Land in the United States," Agricultural Economic Report No. 247, 1969, p. v.

2. Special Issue "Endangered Species," *National Wildlife* (April-May 1974):6, 29.

3. Paul C. Glick and Arthur J. Norton, "Perspectives on the Recent Upturn in Divorce and Remarriage," *Demography* 10, 3 (August 1973):301-314.

4. U.S. Bureau of the Census, "Mobility of Population in the United States March 1970-March 1971," Current Population Report Series P-23, #273, 1971.

5. Aldo Leopold, *A Sand County Almanac* (New York: Oxford University Press, 1974), p. 203.

6. Ibid., p. 204.

7. Ibid., pp. 224-225.

8. Dennis and Donella Meadows et al., *The Limits To Growth* (New York: Universe Books, 1972).

9. Quoted in E.F. Schumacher *Small Is Beautiful* (New York: Harper Torchbooks, 1973), p. 22.

10. E.F. Schumacher, "Modern Pressures and the Environment," *The Journal of The Soil Association*, December 1973, p. 2.

11. *New York Times Magazine*, September 12, 1970.

12. *Business and Society Review* Interview, "Milton Friedman Responds," Spring 1972, pp. 6-7.

13. Louis B. Lundborg, *Future Without Shock* (New York: W.W. Norton, 1974), p. 84.

14. Ibid.

15. Ibid., pp. 128-129.

16. Abraham Maslow, *Motivation and Personality* (New York: Harper & Row, 1954).

Part II. The Evolution of Environmental Ethics

17. Theodore Roosevelt, "Opening Address by the President," in Roderick Nash *The American Environment: Readings in the History of Conservation* (Menlo Park, Calif.: Addison-Wesley, 1968), p. 50.

18. Ibid., p. 52.

19. Aldo Leopold, *Game Management* (New York: Charles Scribner's, 1947), p. 13.

20. Roderick Nash, *The American Environment: Readings in the History of Conservation* (Menlo Park, Calif.: Addison-Wesley, 1968), p. xv.

21. Ezekiel 34:2.

22. Luke 6:31.

23. *The Best Nature Writing of Joseph Wood Krutch* (New York: Morrow, 1969), p. 383.

24. *The American Environment: Readings in the History of Conservation*, p. 9.

25. John Ise, *Our National Park Policy A Critical History* (Maryland: Johns Hopkins Press, 1967), p. 16.

26. *The American Environment*, p. 18.

27. Ibid., p. xv.

28. Ibid., p. xvi.

29. Paul W. Gates, *The History of Public Land Law Development* (Washington, D.C.: U.S. Government Printing Office, 1968), pp. 181, 321-334.

30. George Perkins Marsh, *Man and Nature*, edited by David Lowenthal (Cambridge, Mass.: Harvard University Press, 1965).

31. Ibid., p. 96.

32. Donald Fleming, "Roots of the New Conservation Movement," in *Perspectives in American History*, Vol. VI, edited by Donald Fleming and Bernard Bailyn (Cambridge, Mass.: Harvard University Press, 1972), p. 23.

33. In Joseph Wood Krutch, *The Best Nature Writing of Joseph Wood Krutch* (New York: Morrow, 1969), p. 378.

34. "Roots of the Conservation Movement," pp. 9, 10.

35. *The American Environment*, p. 28.

36. *Man's Dominion*, p. 74.

37. Ibid., p. 110.

38. *The American Environment*, p. 39.

39. Ibid., p. 92.

40. Ibid., p. xvi.

41. *Our National Park Policy*, p. 193.

42. *The American Environment*, p. xviii.

43. "National Wildlife," 13, 1 (December-January 1975):3.

44. *A Sand County Almanac*, p. 203.

45. Ibid., p. 210.

46. Ibid., p. 214.

47. Ecological Society of America, *Directory of Members* 54, 3a (1973):3.

48. In *The Subversive Science*, edited by Paul Shepard and Daniel McKinley (New York: Houghton Mifflin, 1969), p. v.

49. Rachael Carson, *Silent Spring* (New York: Houghton Mifflin, 1962).

50. Garrett Hardin, *Exploring New Ethics for Survival*, (New York: Viking, 1972), pp. 250-263.

51. *The Use of Land*, edited by William K. Reilly (New York: Crowell, 1973).

52. Opinion Research Corporation of Princeton, N.J., *Public Opinion Index* 33, 16 (End August 1975).

53. Ibid.

Part III. Environmental Choices

54. Leonard Lund, *Corporate Organization for Environmental Policymaking* (New York: The Conference Board, 1974), pp. 2-4.

55. *New York Times*, October 2, 1974, "Industry Doubts Threat to Ozone."

56. *New York Times*, September 10, 1975, Walter Sullivan, "Satellite's Scannings Back Theory on Peril to Ozone," pp. 1, 21.

57. *New York Times*, June 22, 1975, Steven Greenhouse, "Aerosol Feels the Ozone Effect," p. 3.

58. Ibid.

59. *Nature Conservancy News*, Release #37074, June 28, 1974.

60. *Nature Conservancy News*, Release #50-74, November 2, 1974.

61. *Nature Conservancy News*, Release #21-73, November 8, 1973.

62. Justice Steward, "Opinion Sierra Club vs. Morton," in Christopher Stone, *Do Trees Have Standing* (Los Altos, Calif.: Kaufmann, 1974), pp. 60-61.

63. *Do Trees Have Standing*, p. 90.

64. Ibid., p. 94.

65. Ibid., p. 68.

66. Ibid., pp. 74-75.

67. Ibid., p. 83.

68. Fred Bosselman and David Callies, *The Quiet Revolution in Land Use Control*, Council on Environmental Quality (Washington, D.C.: U.S. Government Printing Office, 1971), p. 188.

69. Maine Bankers Association, "Bankers Pollution Code," Augusta, Maine, 1970.

70. Ibid., pp. 1-2.

71. Editor Luna Leopold, *Round River from the Journals of Aldo Leopold* (New York: Oxford Press, 1953), pp. 156-157.

II Key Problems in World Population

Michael S. Teitelbaum

In seeking to deal with the issue of world population and its relationships with other world problems, the Commission on Critical Choices for Americans need be under no illusions as to the nature of the beast which it is confronting. The importance of population can be (and has been) overdone, but it is no exaggeration to say that it poses perhaps *the most complex, intractable, and fundamental long-term problems facing humankind today.* This description is not employed lightly out of an affection for hyperbole; it is the plain and uncompromising truth. In dealing with the issue of population, the Commission has indeed chosen an area of critical choices, not only for America, but for the species as a whole.

Current Status and Trends

This review of the current status of population problems will focus both upon the aggregation of world population and upon the specific case of the United States. The situations in the world as a whole and in the United States differ markedly, a point which is often glossed over in discussions of "the population problem."

For the world as a whole, the current population situation is unique in the entire experience of mankind. The present population of the world is the highest in history, about four billion, and the growth rate of the population is also at its highest level. This means that the number of persons added each year to the

49

human population (the product of the population size times the growth rate) is literally extraordinary—between seventy-five and eighty million people per year, and equal to the combined populations of France, Belgium and the Netherlands today, or perhaps one-third of the entire world's population at the beginning of the Christian era.

For nearly the entirety of mankind's existence, human population grew at an annual rate averaging very close to zero. For example, in the 10,000 years from about 10,000 B.C. to 1 A.D., the estimated human population increased by about 245 million, from about 5 million to about 250 million. A similar increase in world population now takes place in just over three years.

The causes of the rapid acceleration in the rate of population growth are by now well known. The first countries to experience this acceleration were the then-developing countries of eighteenth and nineteenth century Europe and North America. As the processes of modernization, industrialization, and urbanization were experienced in these countries, their death rates began to decline, while their birthrates remained at the high levels of the past. The causes of the mortality decline are variously attributed to improved sanitation and health measures, to new and more productive agricultural crops, to the reduction of localized famine via improved communication and transport of foodstuffs, and to generalized improvements in standards of living.

A macro-historical view would hold that the above mortality decline was generally followed by a fertility decline, although there was usually a long lag between these which resulted in a period of rapid demographic growth. The causes of this fertility decline are even more in dispute than the causes of the mortality decline. Factors such as urbanization, industrialization, modernization, compulsory education, declining infant mortality, and even a growth in "rationality" and "hope" are variously employed to explain the fertility decline. Yet, such a broad historical view tends to be misleading for policy purposes. In some European countries fertility began to decline at the same time or even before the decline in mortality—for example, in France. In other cases the fertility decline lagged behind the mortality decline by nearly a century—for example, in England. Careful and intensive analysis of European population data from the nineteenth and twentieth centuries reveals that there are no clear uniformities in the pattern and timing of declines of either fertility or mortality. Satisfying scientific explanations of these trends are not forthcoming from the use of supposed causal variables such as urbanization, education, proportion of women in the labor force, ethnic characteristics of the population, infant mortality, etc.

At present, fertility in developed countries is everywhere low and generally declining; in many such countries, including the United States, fertility levels are currently below replacement level and at all-time historical lows. It must not be overlooked, however, that population continues to grow at nonnegligible rates in most of these countries, due to the substantial momentum for further growth which is incorporated into their age structures as a consequence of their recent history of growth. In addition, the level of fertility in a given year is highly volatile in countries in which most of the population practices effective means of fertility control. The paradox here is that the greater the rational individual control of fertility, the less our ability to predict the course of aggregate fertility. Hence no one can predict the future of fertility trends in these countries; it is equally likely that in the short term fertility levels will continue to decline or will increase, and in the long term they are likely to fluctuate, perhaps dramatically.

One disturbing aspect of population trends in developed countries is a growing propensity among some groups in many of these countries to become concerned by their historically low levels of fertility. It appears to be all too easy for uninformed persons to misinterpret the meaning of below-replacement fertility to mean actual population decline. The fact that population growth has been the normal situation for the entirety of modern history in these countries means that population stability has come to be considered "abnormal," and, indeed, that population decline might be considered "threatening."

In response to some of the irrational responses to low levels of fertility, many developed countries have considered or have actually taken measures intended to raise the level of fertility. The most dramatic case was that of Romania, which in 1966 implemented a set of draconian population policies aimed at sharply increasing fertility levels. In a country in which an estimated 95 percent of women of reproductive age depended upon legal abortion for fertility control, abortion was abruptly declared illegal with few exceptions. The importation of oral contraceptives and intrauterine devices was banned. A substantial tax surcharge was applied to unmarried and/or childless adults, while a comparable tax reduction was offered to families with three or more children. Direct incentives favoring larger families were established, including birth bonuses, increased maternity leave, and early retirement for mothers of three or more children. Finally, an extensive propaganda program was established, including Mother Heroine awards for women with eight or more children, radio interviews with doctors asserting that women in their late 40s took no risk in pregnancy, and interviews with lonely old people bemoaning their youthful folly in having only one child, now deceased.

The results of this demographic overkill were, to say the least, dramatic; the Romanian population experienced what must be the sharpest increase in fertility in the history of the species. All measures of fertility increased by about 100 percent in the single year from 1966 to 1967, and on a month-to-month basis the birthrate increased by 200 percent. Overcrowding of maternity facilities, and a bitterly ironic shortage of medical personnel (many of whom were women and on maternity leave) resulted in soaring rates of maternal and infant mortality.

The Romanian case is an extreme one; no other developed country has taken such measures to raise fertility. But the fact remains that many developed countries continue to view their low fertility rates with concern and in some cases even alarm, and a number have adopted policies explicitly directed to raise the average number of births per woman.

The population situation of the presently developing countries differs both quantitatively and qualitatively from the experience of the presently industrialized countries. The decline in mortality in modern developing countries began only four or five decades ago, and it has been far more precipitous than the earlier decline in Europe. This great success of modern developing countries in rapidly reducing their mortality rates is due more to the importation and rapid implementation of public health measures than to social and economic development. At the same time, birthrates in the developing countries have been and continue to be substantially higher than those even in preindustrial Europe, due primarily to the prevalence of earlier and more nearly universal marriage in the modern developing countries. The result has been rapid population growth rates which dwarf the previously unprecedented rates of nineteenth century Europe. Some developing countries are currently experiencing growth rates approaching 3.5 percent; and the average of all developing countries (including those which have experienced unmistakable fertility declines in the last few years) is still about 2.5 percent, which is more than three times higher than that of nineteenth century Europe.

At the same time, however, there have been modest signs of a quickened pace of fertility decline in developing countries as compared to the fertility declines in the nineteenth century. At least a dozen developing countries of small to moderate size can document a substantial decline in birthrates only a few decades after the onset on substantial declines in mortality. These include Hong Kong, Singapore, Taiwan, South Korea, Sri Lanka, West Malaysia, Barbados, Chile, Costa Rica, Trinidad and Tobago, Jamaica, Puerto Rico, Mauritius, Egypt, and Tunisia. There is further evidence of a possible decline in fertility for another half dozen or so countries, including large ones such as China and Brazil.

The causes of the fertility decline in the developing countries described above is much in dispute. Some argue that these declines are merely a twentieth century repetition of the phenomenon of the European Demographic Transition. These advocates point out that most of the countries with clear declines in fertility have experienced rapid economic development, industrialization, and urbanization, and they argue that these socioeconomic forces have caused the declines in birthrates. Others point to the extensive and intensive population and family planning programs in most of these countries and argue that their declines in birthrates may be explained at least in part in terms of the high effectiveness and acceptability of these programs.

Whatever may be the sources of these fertility declines, and even if they continue and fertility reaches the low levels of developed countries, the populations of the developing world will continue to grow for many decades to come. Rapid population growth in the recent past implies a strong *momentum* for further growth in the future. First, the pro-natalist pressures which maintained high fertility are well established and cannot be eliminated overnight; changes in these social forces can take many decades. Second, a rapidly growing population generates a "young" age structure, that is, one with a large proportion of children and adolescents. As these young enter the reproductive ages there inevitably will be more potential parents.

The power of this momentum factor may be illustrated by applying the highly unrealistic assumption that fertility in developing countries would decline to the "replacement" level now characteristic of developed countries within the next *decade* (i.e., by 1980 to 1985). Even under this assumption, the population of the developing world would nonetheless continue to grow for sixty to seventy years, and would eventually reach a size fully 88 percent greater than its 1970 level (see Table II-1).

Under the more realistic assumption that fertility in developing countries will decline to "replacement" level by 2000 to 2005 (this would still represent a rapid fertility decline when compared to the experience of Europe), the eventual growth from 1970 levels would be 158 percent for the developing world, 123 percent for the world as a whole, and as high as 248 percent and 229 percent for Bangladesh and Mexico, respectively.

Hence population growth rates, unlike many other societal rates, are not

Table II-1
Future Population Growth

Area/ Country	Population* circa 1970	Eventual population* size if replacement by		Percent increase from 1970 level if replacement by	
		1980-85	2000-05	1980-85	2000-05
World	3,652	6,245	8,135	+71	+123
Developing World	2,530	4,763	6,525	+88	+158
China	734	1,270	1,622	+73	+121
India	534	1,002	1,366	+88	+156
Brazil	94	192	266	+104	+183
Bangladesh	69	155	240	+125	+248
Nigeria	65	135	198	+108	+205
Pakistan	57	112	160	+96	+181
Mexico	51	111	168	+118	+229
Philippines	38	79	119	+108	+213
Egypt	34	64	92	+88	+171

*(in millions)

Source: Adapted from Tomas Frejka, Reference Tables to *The Future Population Growth: Alternative Paths to Equilibrium* (New York: The Population Council, 1973).

subject to short- or even medium-term governmental manipulation. All developing countries are assured (barring catastrophe) of very large population increases no matter what the course of fertility, for the next 75 to 125 percent increase is *already* built into their age structures.

Critical Problems in Population

By now there is no serious disagreement as to the inevitability of stabilization of population growth in the long term. The alternative of continued population growth in a finite world is a logical absurdity.[a] However, there is great disagreement as to the importance of reductions in the rate of population growth in the near and medium term for the well-being of the world and of the developing world in particular, and as to responsibility for necessary actions. The key questions of disagreement are as follows:

1. What ultimate population size can the world support in an adequate fashion and what size is desirable on grounds of human values?
2. By what process will population growth decline and eventually cease?
3. What need is there for efforts directed specifically toward reducing population growth as contrasted with general economic and social development?
4. Whose responsibility is it to accommodate inevitable population growth and take actions necessary to reduce future growth?

There is little, if any, agreement as to the population size which can be effectively supported by the resources of the world. The concept of "biological carrying capacity" is heuristically useful, but quantitatively unspecifiable. Some argue that the carrying capacity of the world has already been exceeded with the present population of about four billion. Others argue that the carrying capacity of the world is well in excess of thirty-five to forty billion, although these calculations intentionally exclude questions such as capital requirements, organizational and technical skill factors, and political considerations. With a range of disagreement of this order of magnitude, discussions of whether or not the world is overpopulated at any particular level are rarely productive.

---

[a]A continuation of the present two percent annual growth rate would imply that:

- In just over 300 years, world land area would have the population density of New York City today;
- In 600 years, there would be one person per square meter of land area;
- In 1,200 years, the weight of world population would be greater than the mass of the earth;
- In 6,500 years, the earth would be a solid sphere of live human bodies expanding outward at the radial velocity of the speed of light.

The point of these mathematical gymnastics is simply to demonstrate that the continuation of current growth rates into the long term is not a logical possibility.

The question of what population size is *desirable* on grounds of human values is also not answerable on the basis of scientific evidence. Each person and each country may have individual views of this, and eventually, such matters will have to be resolved via the political process. However, it is difficult to identify any human values which would be furthered by substantial growth beyond the near-doubling which is already mandated by the age structure of most developing countries.

Fortunately, the question of what is a desirable *rate* of increase *is* scientifically answerable. There are no convincing scientific arguments showing that rates of population growth in excess of 1.0 to 1.5 percent contribute positively to development goals, even in countries which are (or believe they are) "underpopulated." The problems of economic and social accommodation to extraordinary and unprecedented growth rates (such as 3.4 percent for Colombia, or 3.2 percent for Kenya) threaten to overwhelm the capacities for accommodation of such countries and to short-circuit the process by which improvements in standard of living, education, etc., are expected to bring about a "natural" fertility decline.

Hence, most agree that population growth must eventually cease, and that the very rapid growth rates of some areas are not beneficial—and all agree that the only humane way to reduce population growth is to reduce fertility. There is much debate, however, as to the nature of the process by which fertility will eventually decline, and the need, or lack thereof, of special governmental efforts to encourage and expedite this decline. The debate is both one of science and of politics, but the political component looms large, as was demonstrated by the World Population Conference in Bucharest.

In the interest of clarifying this debate, I have previously developed a classification of analytically separable positions as indicated below.[1] These must be read with two important *caveats*. First, limitations of space make it inevitable that descriptions of these positions will be oversimplified distillations of what are often subtle and eloquent arguments. Second, it must be noted that these positions are distinct from one another only in analytical terms; in the real world a person or country will usually adopt several of the positions which are mutually supportive of a particular perspective on population issues. A list of extant analytical positions ought to include at least the following:

Positions Against the Need for Special
Population Programs and Policies

1. The Pro-natalist position
   —Rapid population growth in a particular country or region is a positive force on grounds of (a) economic development, in that a larger population provides necessary economies of scale and a sufficient labor supply; (b) pro-

tection of currently underpopulated areas from covetous neighbors; (c) differentials in fertility among ethnic, racial, religious, or political population segments; (d) military and political power and the vitality of a younger age structure.

2. The Revolutionist position
—Population programs are mere palliatives to fundamental social and political contradictions which will inevitably lead to a just revolution, and may therefore be viewed as inherently counterrevolutionary.

3. The Anti-colonial and Genocide positions
—The motives of rich countries which are pushing poor developing countries to adopt aggressive population programs are open to suspicion. These rich countries went through a period of rapid population growth as a component of their own development processes, and their current efforts to restrain population growth in the developing countries are an attempt to maintain the status quo by retarding the development of these countries.
—One can also see the undue emphasis on population as an attempt on the part of the rich developed countries to "buy development cheaply."
—Finally, a person who is very suspicious of the motives of the developed countries could see in their population efforts an attempt to limit or reduce the relative or absolute size of poor and largely nonwhite populations. Such a practice could be seen as a subtle form of genocide deriving from racist or colonialist motives.

4. The Over-consumption position
—So-called "population problems" are actually problems of resource scarcity and environmental deterioration which derive primarily from activities of the rich developed countries, and not from high fertility in the developing countries.
—Even if fertility is too high in the developing countries, this is a consequence of their poverty, which in turn results from over-consumption of the world's scarce resources by rich countries.

5. The Accomodationist position
—As in the past, growing numbers can be readily accommodated by improvements in agricultural and industrial technologies.
—The world has already shown that Malthus' predictions were incorrect; the same is true of the neo-Malthusian predictions and solutions.
—That which is termed "overpopulation" in a given situation is really a matter of underemployment. A humane and properly structured economy can provide employment and the means of subsistence for all people, no matter what the size of the population.

6. The Problem-is-Population-Distribution position

—It is not numbers per se which are causing population problems, but their distribution in space. Many areas of the world (or country) are underpopulated; others have too many people in too small an area.

—Instead of efforts to moderate the rate of numbers growth, governments should undertake efforts to reduce rural-urban flows and bring about a more even distribution of population on the available land.

7. The Mortality and Social Security position

—High fertility is a response to high mortality and morbidity; bring these levels down and fertility will decline naturally.

—Living children are the primary means by which poor people can achieve security in old age. Hence a reduction in infant and child mortality levels or provision of alternative forms of social security would lead to a reduction in fertility.

8. The Status and Roles of Women position

—High fertility levels are perpetuated by norms and practices which define women primarily as procreative agents.

—As long as women's economic and social status depend largely or solely upon the number of children they bear, there is little possibility that societal fertility will decline substantially.

9. The Religious Doctrinal position

—In one form this position holds that population is not a serious problem. Be fruitful and multiply, God will provide.

—In another form this position holds that while current rates of population growth are a serious problem, the primary instruments to deal with them are morally unacceptable, e.g., modern contraception and surgical sterilization are "unnatural," abortion is "murder."

10. The Medical Risk position

—The goal of fertility reduction is not worth the medical risks of the primary instruments of population programs. Oral contraceptives and intrauterine devices have measurable, if small, short-term risks, and some people fear their long-term effects. Sterilization and abortion are operative procedures, all of which have an element of risk, particularly when performed outside the hospital.

11. The Holistic Development position

—Fertility decline is a natural concomitant of social and economic development, as proven by the European Demographic Transition.

—Most of the fertility decline in developing countries with family planning programs therefore derives from the impact of social and economic development rather than from the programs themselves.

—International assistance for development is too heavily concentrated upon population programs, and is short-changing general development programs.

12. The Social Justice position

—Neither population programs nor economic development as presently pursued will bring about necessary fertility declines.

—Fertility will not decline until the basic causes of high fertility—poverty, ignorance, fatalism, etc.—are eliminated through social policies which result in a redistribution of power and wealth among the rich and poor, both within and among nations.

Positions Supporting the Need for Special
Population Programs and Policies:

1. The Population Hawk position

—Unrestrained population growth is the principal cause of poverty, malnutrition, environmental disruption, and other social problems. Indeed, we are faced with impending catastrophe on food and environmental fronts.

—Such a desperate situation necessitates draconian action to restrain population growth, even if coercion is required. "Mutual coercion, mutually agreed upon."

—Population programs are fine as far as they go, but they are wholly insufficient in scope and strength to meet the desperate situation.

2. The Provision of Services position

—Surveys and common sense show that there is a great unmet demand for fertility control in all countries; hence the main problem is to provide modern fertility control to already motivated people.

—Some proponents also hold that the failure of some service programs is due to inadequate fertility control technologies, and that the need for technological improvements is urgent.

3. The Human Rights position

—As recognized in the United Nations Tehran Declaration (1968), it is a fundamental human right for each person to be able to determine the size of his or her own family.

—Furthermore, some argue that each woman has the fundamental right to the control of her own bodily processes. (This position usually leads to support for abortion as well as contraception.)

—Health is also a basic human right, which population programs help to achieve through a variety of direct and indirect pathways, including the direct medical benefits of increased child spacing on maternal and child health, and the indirect effects of reducing the incidence of dangerous illegal abortions.

4. The Population-Programs-Plus-Development position

—Social and economic development are necessary but not sufficient to bring about a new equilibrium of population at low mortality and fertility levels. Special population programs are also required.

—Too rapid population growth is a serious intensifier of other social and economic problems, and is one, though only one, of a number of factors behind lagging social and economic progress in many countries.

—Some countries might benefit from larger populations, but would be better served by moderate rates of growth over a longer period than by very rapid rates of growth over a shorter period.

—An effective population program therefore is an essential component of any sensible development program.

At Bucharest these analytically separable positions found their expression in a variety of combinations representing diverse perspectives of the relationship between population and development. The most important combinations were:

1. *Holistic Development (Especially Via the Establishment of a "New International Economic Order") Plus Anti-Colonial Plus Over-Consumption.* This combination of positions was held by a large group of countries (indeed, the majority of the conference participants). Some of these were also supporters of a Pro-natalist position at the same time, but others disagreed and expressed concern about rapid population growth. In the former category were such countries as Algeria, Argentina, China, Albania, Romania (the conference host), Cuba, Peru, and many countries of Francophone Sub-Saharan Africa. In the latter category were such countries as India, Mexico, Egypt, Yugoslavia, Italy, and some Latin American and African states.

2. *Population Programs Plus Development.* This position was generally supported by most of the developing countries of Asia (excluding China and India) and by most of the developed countries outside the Socialist bloc. It was the position supported by governments representing a majority of the *people* of the developing world, excluding China, but only a minority of the *countries* of this group.

3. *Traditional Marxian (With Elements of the Accommodationist and Anti-Colonial Positions).* The group of countries holding this position, which included the USSR and most of Eastern Europe (excluding Romania and Yugoslavia) held that there is no such thing as a "population problem" in the abstract. Each mode of production (feudalism, capitalism, socialism) has its own laws of population, and the so-called population problems of the Third World are a component of

the capitalist mode, resulting from colonialism, neo-colonialism, and imperialism. Hence, according to this view, there is no need for population policies per se, for in a properly organized world and society, the demographic trends are adjusted automatically by social and economic forces. What *is* required is the transformation of the world order to allow this "natural" process to take place.

Perhaps the most interesting political grouping in the conference was that of eight countries whose numerous amendments dominated the first week of discussion on the World Plan of Action. Most of this group's amendments had the effect of deleting specific references to population problems and population policies, substituting instead references to the need for social and economic development and a new international economic order. The group included Argentina (which has recently adopted one of the world's most strongly pro-natalist population policies) as well as India and Egypt (both of which have established national policies aimed at reducing fertility levels.) India and Egypt may have been seeking to play a "bridging" function between the divergent Third World views on population. Nonetheless, the participation of India in this group was in sharp contrast to the views of most of her Asian neighbors. Other members of the eight-nation group were Ethiopia, Italy, Lesotho, Liberia, and Yugoslavia.

The posture of China was also of considerable interest. The Chinese delegation was one of the first to publicly attack the draft Plan of Action as inappropriately concentrated upon demographic variables and lacking in emphasis upon the need for a New International Economic Order which would eliminate the effects of "imperialism, colonialism, neo-colonialism, and hegemonism." The rapid population growth of the Third World was "a very good thing" according to the Chinese delegation, since it had allowed these countries to become the main force opposing the domination of the Super Powers. The idea of a population explosion was an "absurd theory concocted by the Super Powers" in order to maintain their hegemony; the real need was to "smash the old economic order" and establish the new. The delegation referred only infrequently to China's widespread program of "birth planning," and emphasized that the goals of this program were to raise fertility in some sectors of the population as well as to lower fertility in others. In the Working Group, the Chinese introduced amendments intended to remove references to fertility reduction.

Meanwhile Brazil, previously one of the most pro-natalist of governments, adopted a posture of support for the draft Plan of Action and did not join actively in the attempts led by Argentina to direct it away from demographic variables and towards development factors. Indeed, the Brazilian delegation chose to announce a change in governmental policy; birth control was a matter of family decision, but it was a state responsibility to provide low-income families with birth control information and services.

Despite the rhetorical bombast of Bucharest, much of which arose from a concern with real problems other than population (such as the drive for the "New International Economic Order"), it is possible to point to a fragile but growing consensus posture, which is based upon the best available evidence and which could form the basis of an informed posture on the part of the United States government. The following are the essentials of its key elements:

1. Population growth is not the only, or even the primary, source of the poverty, disease, illiteracy, and gross inequality which now characterize the world. The ultimate solution to such problems depends on the true social and economic development of the poor countries of the world, and this cannot be "bought cheaply" through definition of population as the major problem.

2. The population problem is not uniform throughout the world, nor can a single characterization be correctly applied to all countries or even to all developing countries. In some regions it is evident that the population is already too large for indigenous resources, while in others resources are available in abundance and development might be served by substantial population increase. It must also be noted that many of the problems arising from large population concentrations derive from patterns of population distribution and migration, as well as from rates of population growth.

3. Nevertheless, it is clear that a very rapid rate of population growth tends to be a negative factor for the prospects of true social and economic development. While reduction of excessively high population growth rates are by no means sufficient to bring about such development, such very rapid growth rates as characterize many developing countries today stand as serious impediments to such progress.

4. The above is true both in areas in which population size is already taxing available resources (e.g., Bangladesh and India) *and* in those areas which could possibly benefit from substantial population increases (e.g., Brazil and some African countries). In the former case, both the absolute size of the population and its rate of increase pose vexatious problems for policymakers, while in the latter case, the very rapid rate of increase presents serious difficulties of accommodation over a short span of time.

5. Hence in all developing countries with very rapid rates of population increase, efforts to moderate these rates are necessary (but *not* sufficient) components of development programs.

6. In none of these cases can a realistic goal be the immediate cessation of population growth, for the momentum of population growth makes such a goal essentially unattainable. Barring catastrophe, the world population and, particularly those of the developing countries, will increase dramatically no matter what population policies are adopted. Hence the world's technological and economic resources must be mobilized to assure that these sharply increased numbers will be accommodated with necessary services and pro-

vided with opportunities for lives of dignity. Indeed, the recognition of this momentum factor is itself a positive argument for early attention to population policies, even in those countries which look forward enthusiastically to substantial further growth.

7. Hence policies and programs are required both for general development and for specific population concerns, and these intrinsically complementary efforts must be components of all development plans and all international development assistance.

This consensus view is increasingly popular among professionals dealing with development and population issues, but it was obviously not the majority position in Bucharest. In large part, this may be attributed to the *political* nature of the conference and of the delegations sent by member states. Professionals were often present in advisory roles only and had little impact upon their governments' official positions. In contrast, the discussions at the three regional preparatory conferences which preceded the Bucharest gathering were attended primarily by delegations composed of professionals, and the discussions were far less political and considerably more constructive. In some individual cases, e.g., Argentina, the official position taken at the Bucharest Conference differed very substantially indeed from the official positions taken at the preparatory conference.

Finally, there remains the question posed earlier: *Whose* responsibility is it to accommodate to inevitable population growth and to take actions necessary to reduce future growth? Are these matters of national sovereignty or do they transcend national boundaries? Such a question was a fundamental one for consideration at the Bucharest Conference, but, unfortunately, the declarations which developed were inconsistent. On the one hand, the conference emphasized the *responsibility* of the developed countries and the newly-rich developing countries to assist the rest in accommodating their population growth and furthering their development efforts. This included specific calls for reduced consumption of food and raw materials by the developed countries. These responsibilities should fall under the rubric of the New International Economic Order adopted by the Sixth Special Session of the United Nations General Assembly, the provisions of which include:[2]

1. An end to all forms of foreign occupation and alien domination and exploitation;
2. A "just and equitable relationship" between prices that developing countries receive for their raw products and the prices they must pay for imported goods;
3. Net transfer of real resources from developed to developing countries, including increases in the real price of commodities exported by developing countries;

4. Improved access to markets in developed countries through a system of preferences for exports of developing countries and through the elimination of tariff and nontariff barriers and restrictive business practices;
5. Reimbursement to developing countries of customs duties and taxes imposed by importing developed countries;
6. Arrangements to mitigate the effects of inflation on developing countries and to eliminate the instability of the world monetary system;
7. Promotion of foreign investment in developing countries in accordance with their needs and requirements;
8. Formulation of an international code of conduct regulating the activities of transnational corporations;
9. Measures to promote the processing of raw materials in the producer developing countries;
10. An increase in essential inputs for food production, including fertilizers, from developed countries on favorable terms;
11. Urgent measures to alleviate the burden of external debt.

On the other hand, issues of population policy were repeatedly declared by the Bucharest Conference to be quintessentially sovereign in nature, with no interference from other nations or international bodies to be allowed. Hence according to the Bucharest pronouncements, the accommodation to population growth is an international responsibility of the rich countries, as is their contribution to development efforts, but the development of population policies is a matter of national sovereignty.

Such a perspective raises important questions of policy for the United States government. In particular:

1. Do food exporting countries, and hence particularly the United States, have a *responsibility* to provide the rest of the world with the food resources they need? What would be the international and domestic ramifications, both economic and political, of actions in this area?
2. Is there a basic human *right* to emigrate from areas of poverty and famine to areas of excess food and resources, even if this means migration into other countries?
3. Does the high consumption level in developed countries of food and raw materials have significant effects, either negative or positive, upon the well-being of the rest of the world? Does this high consumption level mean that the low population growth rates of these countries pose as serious a "population problem" as the high population growth rates of the lower-consumption countries?
4. In an age of growing "interdependence" of world economies, to what extent are population policies actually sovereign?

Objectives for U.S. Policy in World Population
for the Years 1985 and 2000

Logically prior to examining objectives for U.S. policy in the population field is the question whether the United States *ought* to have a policy in this area. It is often forgotten that in 1958 President Eisenhower was quoted as saying: "I cannot imagine anything more emphatically a subject that is not a proper political or governmental activity or function or responsibility . . . As long as I am here this government will not have a positive political doctrine on birth control."

The rapid growth of U.S. governmental sophistication and awareness of the fundamental nature of population issues may be measured by the fact that just over a decade later the United States is the most generous supporter of population activities all over the world. But what are the U.S. interests—both self-interests and altruistic interests? Does it really matter to the American taxpayer whether the population of Bangladesh triples, or whether there is a massive famine in India? Like all issues of foreign policy, the answers to such questions may be viewed from a variety of perspectives, including issues of international politics, economic impacts, and universal morality. Indeed, each of these types of factors interact with the others. One way to examine such a complex play of forces is to imagine alternative futures of population growth and seek to explore the implications of these alternatives from the various points of view.

In so doing, we must first reiterate that under no circumstances, barring catastrophe, will the populations of the developing world cease to grow before they have increased by about 90 percent from 1970 levels. Indeed, this is a highly unlikely alternative future, for it would require a nearly-immediate (specifically by 1980 to 1985) decline of their fertility to the levels of the most advanced of developed countries. A more plausible, though still optimistic, eventuality would be additional growth of about 160 percent from 1970 levels, with a gradual decline of fertility (or an increase of mortality) to reach replacement levels by the period 2000 to 2005. If this were to be achieved primarily via a fertility decline, it would likely require the most strenuous and effective efforts of governments and international assistance in the history of the world. A pessimistic alternative would be for fertility not to come into balance with mortality until the periods 2020-2025 or even 2040-2045, resulting respectively in eventual increases of about 275 percent and 450 percent from 1970 levels.

Given the present world shortages and prices of foodstuffs, energy and fertilizers, it is clear that even the optimistic alternative of "only" nearly 90 percent increases in the populations of developing countries will impose notable strains upon their own and others' capacities to provide the means of subsistence. This is not put forward as a simplistic Malthusian argument. With the benefit of hindsight we know that Malthus was wrong in 1798 when he predicted that humankind had a greater short-term potential for procreation than did agriculture for increased production. Since Malthus' time, the growth of food production has if anything exceeded that of population. Yet, much of this growth was dependent in effect upon the conversion of the energy of fossil fuels into edible grains via the process of plant photosynthesis. While the engine of this process is the sun, fertilizers derived from oil, gas, and coal are one of its basic raw materials. The present shortages of these energy sources (whether real or manipulated) and high prices (obviously manipulated) have, for the first time, placed substantial barriers in the way of this conversion process, barriers which are exacerbated by the numerous political and economic problems associated with the current world energy situation.

As we have said, it is certain that even under the most optimistic (and quite unrealistic) projection of a virtually immediate decline in fertility in the developing world to "replacement" level, the momentum for further growth built into their age structures will require the development of food resources for a near doubling of their numbers to nearly five billion in about sixty to seventy years. Since technological, not to mention economic, forecasting has a notoriously bad performance record, it would be presumptuous here to forecast that continued and stable increases in food production to levels double those at present by 2050 cannot be achieved. While it is clear that such increases will not be easy, they are possible given strenuous effort and adequate investment, particularly in the productive resources of the developing countries themselves. The current political and economic situation of the world does not make one sanguine that these will be forthcoming, particularly given the shortage of capital in many Western industrialized countries and the apparent unwillingness of capital-surplus countries to assume the risks of direct investments in the poorest of the developing nations. Achieving necessary increases will thus be a major triumph of international diplomacy even under the most optimistic of the alternative population futures.

When the second demographic alternative is considered, that of a 160 percent increase in the developing world populations, the prognosis becomes more disturbing. Based upon past experience, the prospect of serious shortfalls in food production in the developing countries cannot be dismissed. As the primary producer and leading exporter of foodstuffs, the United States would in this circumstance face a fundamental dilemma—fundamental on grounds of politics, economics, and ethics. In political terms, the refusal by the United States to make up food deficits at concessionary rates could easily lead to critical instabilities in areas such as South Asia, a region which over the coming years may become the first area of widespread nuclear proliferation. On economic grounds, however, the growing importance to the American economy of food exports, both in terms of the balance of payments and domestic price inflation, would militate against large-scale export of foodstuffs at concessionary prices.

The inability of prospective food-deficit countries to pay market prices for food imports would therefore require financing of such purchases by the newly rich OPEC countries (an unlikely development) or self-financing by the United States with consequent deleterious effects upon her balance of payments. Finally, on ethical and humanitarian grounds, the American people will not face with equanimity the prospect of widespread famine in large sectors of the world's population, particularly when the United States may, at the same time, be the primary food surplus country. A choice to allow the "free-market" forces to control allocations of U.S. food surpluses (as per present administration policy) would in effect deny surplus U.S. food to those countries most needing it in favor of those best able to pay.

Such dilemmas are magnified by several orders of magnitude under the final set of pessimistic demographic projections described above. Under such circumstances, it is difficult to see how U.S. policy could meet burgeoning demand for food on a continuous basis, especially given the cyclicity of North American climatological conditions. While utter despair would not be appropriate under such circumstances, the prognosis clearly would not be an encouraging one.

A final note is in order on the plausibility of the above demographic projections. All assume that mortality conditions will not materially worsen (indeed that they will improve somewhat) in developing countries over the course of the projections. The alternative of modern developing countries developing a new, and perverse, form of the Demographic Transition cannot, however, be completely discounted. It is possible, for example, that instead of a gradual decline in fertility to levels eventually consistent with low fertility/low mortality replacement, some developing countries might experience both a slow decline in fertility *and* a gradual increase in mortality, resulting eventually in an equilibrium state of moderate fertility/moderate mortality. There is already some fragmentary and inconclusive evidence of small mortality increases in South Asia, particularly in Bangladesh and parts of India. These increases, if real, may represent temporary aberrations in the long-term trend of declining mortality, but they may also be the first signs of things to come. We shall be able to know for sure only with the 20/20 vision of hindsight.

In general the objectives of U.S. policy on population must focus upon, and ideally would be perceived by others to be concerned with, the improvement of the quality of life for the world as a whole, and especially the lives of that majority of humankind living in developing countries. By definition, then, population policy includes necessary efforts to reduce levels of mortality and morbidity, as well as efforts to bring fertility and population growth rates down to levels which can be accommodated with necessary food, housing, and other social services. Fundamentally these objectives fall into three broad categories:

1. Accommodation;
2. Achievement of desired fertility control; and,
3. Encouragement of motivation for smaller families.

These different objectives require different approaches, and indeed they may be viewed as a temporal sequence to be confronted sequentially over the coming decades.

Accommodation. The momentum for future population growth, which is already incorporated into the age structure of most developing countries, means that no matter what happens to fertility over the coming decades and barring catastrophe, very substantial growth will be experienced. In some large developing countries, such as Bangladesh, Nigeria, Mexico, and the Philippines, the strength of the demographic momentum is such that growth under such circumstances would be well over 200 percent. There is no humane alternative to finding a way to accommodate to this magnitude of growth. This will require strenuous efforts to increase the production of foodstuffs, clothing, housing and employment in virtually every developing country.

Achievement of Desired Fertility Control. The goal of achieving reliable control of fertility down to levels desired by the population is the same goal which implicitly underlies domestic U.S. population "policy."[b] It amounts to the provision of sufficient information and services to eliminate unwanted fertility. Available data suggests that there is extensive unwanted fertility in virtually every developing country. Most persons in developing countries do not have easy access to modern methods of fertility control for reasons of either ignorance, economic deprivation or simple inaccessability of services. The provision of safe and effective methods of fertility control to all who desire them is a basic principle of all population programs and ought to be pursued strenuously, with due attention to the enormous management difficulty of such programs in the context of many developing country situations.

In this regard it is notable that our present armamentarium of fertility control methods is hardly ideal. All available methods of fertility control carry significant drawbacks, especially in situations in which medical personnel are in severe shortage. For example, the IUD is a method with considerable difficulties (side effects and rejection), and competent personnel trained in the appropriate procedures to insure maximum effectiveness of these devices are essential for effectiveness of any programs using them.

The much exaggerated medical risks of oral contraceptives are also real, though small. Extensive prospective studies recently reported by researchers in Great Britain of medical defects of oral contraception demonstrate as conclusively as any medical evidence can that there are no substantial risks to the use of these preparations. In this light, it is a compelling irony that the governments of some countries continue to refuse to license the widespread distribution of oral contraceptives (sometimes even under medical supervision), due to a perceived risk to the health of women in these countries. There are small risks to

bThe United States still has no explicit population policy despite the cogent recommendations of the Commission on Population Growth and the American Future, issued in 1972.

the use of any medical preparation or procedure, but it is an axiom of any evaluation of such risks that they must be considered in relation to the alternative risks. In many developing countries, the mortality risks of a normal pregnancy and especially of higher-order pregnancies are far greater than the risks of the use of oral contraceptives, even in the absence of medical supervision. Indeed, the risk to health of smoking cigarettes is considerably greater than that of the consumption of oral contraceptives. Such a relative perspective is rarely considered in the evaluation of contraceptives for licensing and approval in most countries. One leading medical specialist is fond of noting that on grounds of medical risk the overall health of the world would be substantially improved by putting cigarettes on prescription and oral contraceptives in cigarette machines.

Motivation to Reduce Family Size. The most difficult problem facing population policies and programs is that of affecting the motivation to reduce family size below present levels. There are at least four ways in which motivations regarding fertility may be affected by conscious government policy:[3]

1. Communicate with people in order to influence their demographic behavior in the desired manner: make available factual information about population and fertility-related matters, provide education or enlightenment via the schools, the media, commissions, and so forth, or seek to persuade people through argumentation and exhortation.
2. Change the balance of incentives and disincentives to achieve the desired regulation: raise or lower the cost of having children through such measures as maternity leaves and benefits, family and child allowances, tax benefits or penalties, social security provisions, educational fees, and direct money payments.
3. Shift the weight of social institutions and opportunities in the desired direction: change marital status, the child mortality rate, provision of popular education, status of women, standard of living, and so forth, in the desired direction.
4. Coerce the desired behavior through the power of the state: legislate and enforce the desired behavior through the power of law and its penalties.

Attempts to communicate with people to influence their demographic behavior seems to be minimally effective in the absence of major social changes. Changes in the balance of incentives and disincentives may have some effect, but can become unduly expensive in order to achieve substantial impact. Transformation of social institutions has clear effects ultimately upon fertility motivation, but it is difficult, slow, and, depending on how it is implemented, can be very costly indeed. Finally, coercion is usually morally offensive to a majority of the population, and therefore politically unacceptable. In addition, it is usually almost impossible to administer. It should be added here that family planning programs themselves can often affect motivation toward fertility by legitimizing the smaller family norm and the use of certain forms of fertility control. In country settings with legitimate governments, the establishment of a governmental population policy favoring reduction in fertility can gradually have the effect of changing the status of fertility control methods from taboo to normal.

In seeking to realize these objectives, particularly the motivational ones, U.S. policymakers must recognize that such efforts can have only gradual impact over a long period. Social institutions favoring high levels of fertility have been fundamental components of all societies which have survived up to the modern epoch; changing these institutions cannot take place overnight. Hence this area requires far more patience and tolerance for ambiguity than perhaps any other area of national policy.

Objectives for United States Domestic Policy on Population

The United States is blessed with the excellent and comprehensive report of its Commission on Population and the American Future, which was submitted to President Nixon in 1972. This report appears to have been largely ignored by the Nixon and Ford administrations, though some of its recommendations have been implemented by the Supreme Court and by Congress. These recommendations included:

1. That the United States welcome below-replacement fertility if it comes, and move gradually towards population stabilization.
2. Provision of contraceptive services to all who desire them on a voluntary basis.
3. Legalization of abortion along the lines of the New York State statute.
4. Support for population education in schools and media.
5. Action to limit the flow of illegal immigration.
6. Adoption of national population distribution policies.
7. Establishment of a national institute of population sciences.
8. Devotion of highest priority to research in reproductive science and contraceptive development.

Faced with these and other recommendations, the only response of the Nixon administration was that President Nixon was opposed to abortion and opposed to contraceptives if they were available for teenagers. Of course, this is not the first commission report to be ignored, nor will it be the last. Nonetheless, the American people should give careful thought to the recommendations of the Commission on Population and the American Future. By so doing, this country may be fortunate enough to avoid the irrational responses to low fertility which have afflicted several developed countries, represented in the extreme by Romania.

Alternatives for United States Policy in Population for the Years 1985 and 2000

In discussing alternatives for U.S. policy in world population, a number of criteria must be imposed which sharply limit the scope for action. In the first place, U.S. policy must take account of the *political constraints* upon U.S. action in this field. In many parts of the world, population activities are controversial, to say the least, and insensitive and aggressive policy can only be counterproductive. Second, U.S. policy must be *realistic*, especially given the strength of momentum for further population growth in the world. Third, policy on population must be *coordinated* with other areas of policy including food, health, development assistance, and so on. Fourth, population policy must be aimed at the development of *indigenous solutions*, especially through the development of capacities for analysis of local population situations and for implementation of policies in the developing countries themselves. And fifth and finally, U.S. policy must be sensitive to the *complexities* of population variables, to the *nonuniformity* of population situations in different regions and countries, and to the *fundamental and persistent nature* of social pressures which encourage high fertility.

Given these criteria, the three areas discussed above present important policy alternatives:

Accommodation to Forthcoming Population Growth. As has already been noted, the momentum for population increase on the order of 75 to 125 percent is already built into the age structure of developing countries. Even if fertility in these countries were to decline in a very few years to the "replacement" level (obviously a near-impossibility), growth of such magnitude would still take place before equilibrium could be achieved. This means that whatever population policies are adopted, all developing countries must accommodate very substantial population increases with adequate food, employment, education, and housing. The United States may assist in this accommodation process in a number of areas.

First is in the area of food reserves. The United States is uniquely able to assist in the provision of a "cushion" against sporadic food shortages through maintenance of domestic food reserves, or through contributions to proposed international reserves. It should be recognized that such contributions, given the current low domestic reserves of foodstuffs, may involve reduction of U.S. consumption of certain commodities (such as beef), either via rationing or via price effects. Some of this has already occurred under present policies, but these policies have not been designed to make food available to those most in need of it.

However, there should be no illusions that the United States can "feed the world." Indigenous production of grains and foodstuffs must be increased in

developing countries themselves if any solution other than temporary crisis
management is to be achieved. The United States can contribute substantially to
this process, as it has already done in the past. Continued application of
American agricultural technology to the problems of food production in the
developing countries is an important form of technological assistance which this
country is uniquely able to make. In addition, capital and technology for
fertilizer and insecticide production and for irrigation are important requirements (though in an ideal world much of the capital would be provided by the
newly-rich, oil-producing countries).

In the area of employment, the United States must recognize that the
inevitable growth of population in developing countries will put enormous
burdens upon their economic structures to provide jobs, given the fact in many
of these countries underemployment and unemployment are already endemic. In
its development assistance the United States would be wise to encourage
labor-intensive, rather than capital-intensive, development as a mechanism of
creating such productive employment. Ultimately, of course, the question of
employment is one that can be confronted only by the policies of the developing
countries themselves; outsiders can do little in this area other than to provide
encouragement in the nature of development assistance.

In the area of health, the inevitable growth of populations in developing
countries points increasingly to the need for paramedical delivery systems for
rural populations. Wherever possible this should be tied to family planning
programs.

In the area of education, once again the inevitable growth of the population
of the developing countries will present notable challenges to resources and
ingenuity. U.S. assistance, if it is to be helpful in the most critical areas, ought to
be aimed at primary education, education-for-literacy, and nonformal education,
with consequently lesser emphasis upon university-level training, except in those
areas which are directly related to problems of development.

Finally in the area of housing, again the primary solutions for accommodating
inevitable population growth will have to be indigenous. U.S. contributions can
only be modest, but could perhaps contribute research efforts directed toward
low cost housing technologies in urban areas.

Realization of Existing Desire for Wanted Fertility. As has been noted, there is
extensive evidence of "unwanted" fertility in most developing countries, though
"wanted" fertility levels are still higher than those required for replacement.
Hence, while the reduction or elimination of unwanted fertility would not bring
about sufficient declines in fertility, there is, nonetheless, considerable scope for
action in this area. The problem is essentially one of developing and delivering
the *means* which can effectively achieve desired fertility reduction in the context
of rural, agrarian, and often illiterate societies.

On the technological side, the available means of fertility control are not adequate, especially in developing country situations where medical personnel are in short supply in rural areas. Here is an area for substantial and important American contributions. U.S. scientific capacities could be mobilized to rectify this situation to the extent that science can do so. Available resources for biomedical research in reproductive science and contraceptive development are chronically inadequate. For example, in fiscal 1973, government support for reproductive science and contraceptive development was only $60 million, as compared to $400 million for cancer research alone. It is reasonable to argue that unrestrained population growth is a greater threat to the world order and the survival of the species than is cancer, and therefore the least we could do would be to give research in human reproduction the same priority as we give to research on one group of diseases.

In the area of providing currently available technologies to developing countries in the form of material and commodities, the United States is already doing a good job. Indeed a lower profile and less flamboyance in this area might prove helpful, though funding levels should be continued or increased to keep pace with increasing demands.

Affecting Motivation to Decrease Fertility Levels. In this fundamental area the scope for U.S. action is highly circumscribed. Aggregate fertility levels are the consequence of millions of individual behaviors which are not easily accessible to manipulation. To the extent that they can be affected at all by governments, it must be by indigenous governments rather than by outsiders. The United States can support and encourage such actions; in such support it would help if this country had adopted an official policy of population stabilization.

In support of development of indigenous population policies aimed at affecting fertility motivations, the United States can contribute to the development of local expertise in population matters, particularly in demography and other related social sciences. It can support research into the correlates (and even the "causes") of fertility motivations. To the extent that such research shows that elements, such as reduced infant mortality, improved status of women, social security, etc., affect such motivations, this country may choose to support these elements in both economic and diplomatic terms. (It should be noted that many such policies ought to be supported in their own right whether or not they affect fertility motivation.)

Overall, then, the present population situation facing the world is a fundamental and "underlying" problem, which is characterized by exceptionally long lag times before any impact of policies can be seen. There are *some* areas in which the United States can make substantial contributions, such as assistance in accommodating inevitable growth, research in reproductive science and social science, provision of fertility-related services and supplies, political support for governmental action in the developing countries themselves, and provision of development assistance likely to affect the lives of the rural majority. However, in other areas the United States can have little impact, and these limitations must be recognized. In elaborating policies directed to population problems in the developing world, the United States should "play to strength," seek the most humane solutions, and finally, exercise patience *far* beyond that required for any other world problem.

Notes

1. M.S. Teitelbaum, "Population and Development: Is a Consensus Possible?" *Foreign Affairs*, July 1974. Reprinted by permission from *Foreign Affairs*, July 1974. Copyright 1974 by Council on Foreign Relations, Inc.

2. Reprinted with the permission of the Population Council from "A Report on Bucharest: The World Population Conference and The Population Tribune," by W. Parker Mauldin, Nazli Choucri, Frank W. Notestein, and Michael Teitelbaum, *Studies in Family Planning* 5, No. 12 (December 1974):362.

3. Reprinted with the permission of the Population Council from "World Population: Status Report 1974," by Bernard Berelson, *Reports on Population/Family Planning*, No. 15 (January 1974), p. 26.

III Food and the Growth of Affluence and Population

Harrison Brown

In the two centuries since industrialization based upon steampower became firmly rooted in human culture, there have emerged "rich" nations in which per capita income and consumption have been relatively high and "poor" nations in which per capita income and consumption have been relatively low. For the most part, levels of per capita income and consumption in the poorest countries have been characteristic of those in traditional peasant-village societies. For the greater part of the history of modern industrial civilization, the distribution of income and consumption among the world's people appears to have been a continuum with most persons being very poor, a few being very rich and the rest, numbering more than the rich but fewer than the poor, being somewhere in between. Since World War II, however, a striking pattern has evolved amounting to no less than a fissioning of human society into two quite separate and distinct cultures—the culture of the rich and the culture of the poor, with very few people living between these two extremes.

The evolution of this process is dramatically illustrated by the changing patterns of per capita energy consumption between 1950 and 1970. Figure III-1 shows the numbers of people living at various levels of energy consumption in 1950, 1960, and 1970. The levels of energy consumption, expressed in units of kilograms of coal equivalent per person per year, are shown on a logarithmic scale, in which each step increases by a factor of two.

We clearly see in the figure a general spread in levels of per capita energy consumption in 1950, the emergence of a bimodal distribution by 1960 and the evolution of a very clear bimodal distribution by 1970. (No reasonably

Kilograms of Coal Equivalent
Per person/per year (logarithmic scale)

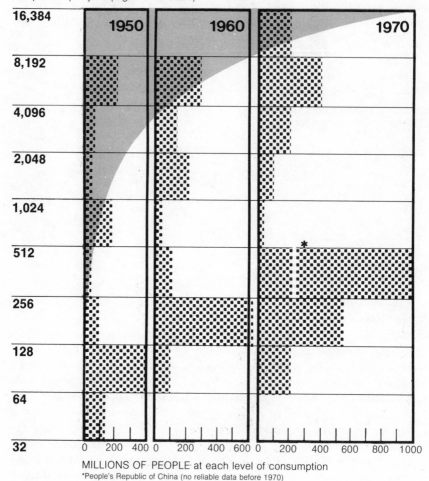

MILLIONS OF PEOPLE at each level of consumption
*People's Republic of China (no reliable data before 1970)

Figure III-1. Per Capita Energy Consumption

authoritative data are available for the People's Republic of China prior to 1970.)

The peaks provide a convenient division of nations into "rich" and "poor" categories. The average characteristics of each category, including the relatively few persons living between the extremes, are shown in Table III-1.

We see from these figures that the rich countries, which have 27 percent of the population of the world account for 84 percent of the world's total energy

Table III-1
Average Population, Energy Consumption, and GNP in 1970

	Rich Nations	Intermediates	Poor Nations
Population (millions)	954	234	2,440
Energy Consumption (millions of mt of coal)	5,680	384	717
Per Capita Energy Consumption (kilograms/person)	5,010	1,610	293
Per Capita GNP (US dollars 1973)	2,720	846	169

consumption. Further, the divergence between the rich and the poor is increasing, largely because of rapid population growth in the latter. In 1960, the average person in a rich country consumed 18.5 times as much energy as a person in a poor country. By 1970, this ratio had grown to 20.5. At current growth rates, the ratio will reach 40:1 by the year 2020.

Table III-2 shows the average growth characteristics of the rich and poor nations together with projections to the year 2020, assuming that current growth rates continue.

Growing affluence in the rich countries is the counterpart of increasing population in the poor countries. When we think of "population," it is misleading to think simply in terms of numbers of people. We must think also in terms of the materials which are associated with an individual, as well as the energy that is required for the individual to function. For example, in a peasant-village society, a typical person might have associated with him a part of a wooden or stone dwelling unit and a few simple tools. He and his possessions will be powered for a year by perhaps 150 kilograms of cereal. By contrast, an average inhabitant of the United States is associated with about 10 tons of steel, 160 kilograms of copper, 140 kilograms of lead, 100 kilograms of zinc, 18 kilograms of tin, and 110 kilograms of aluminum. Instead of living on 150 kilograms of cereal each year, he requires the energy equivalent to burning more than 10 tons of coal.

Clearly something is bound to give long before the year 2020 is reached. Current growth rates simply cannot persist much longer. Of consuming interest is the *manner* in which growth rates will change. Will rates of population growth and per capita consumption change as the result of premeditated, constructive actions on the part of the world's people? Will they change as the result of such factors as malnutrition and disease, environmental degradation, and decreasing resource availability? Will they change as a result of continuing conflict between rich and rich, between poor and poor, and between rich and poor? Or will growth rates change as the result of a major catastrophic world upheaval?

Table III-2
Selected Average Growth Characteristics of Rich and Poor Nations

	Rich Nations	Poor Nations
1970 Population (millions)	954	2,440
Annual Population Growth Rate	0.8%	2.5%
1970 Per Capita Energy Consumption (tons of coal per year)	6.0	0.29
Annual Growth Rate of Energy Consumption	5.2%	5.6%
2020 Population (millions)	1,400	8,500
2020 Per Capita Energy Consumption (tons of coal per year)	54	1.4

Population, Affluence and Demands for Food

The rich nations are characterized by low death rates and by low and decreasing birthrates. Collectively, the 950 million inhabitants of the rich countries are increasing their numbers at the rate of but 0.8 percent per year—smaller than the rate of population growth in the poor countries by a factor of three. High and increasing levels of agricultural production per man-hour worked and per acre farmed have resulted from mechanization (using fossil fuels for energy), liberal application of fertilizers and pesticides, irrigation, and the genetic selection of plant varieties best suited for particular environments.

As agricultural productivity has increased and as industries have been developed, people have migrated from rural to urban areas. Most people now live in or near cities and their proportion appears likely to increase.

As affluence has increased, diets have changed. Generally, rich people eat more animal products than do poor ones. On the average, six to ten plant calories are required to produce an animal calorie in the form of meat, milk or eggs. Per capita cereal consumption in the United States now exceeds 800 kilograms per person, most of which is fed to animals. This is about 4.5 times larger than per capita cereal consumption in India, where most of the grains are eaten directly by people.

There is some evidence that per capita consumption of cereals has stopped increasing in the United States (see Figure III-2). But in other regions of the rich part of the world, notably Europe, the USSR, and Japan, per capita cereal demands are increasing rapidly and might eventually approach that in the United

Kilograms of cereal per year (includes animal feed)

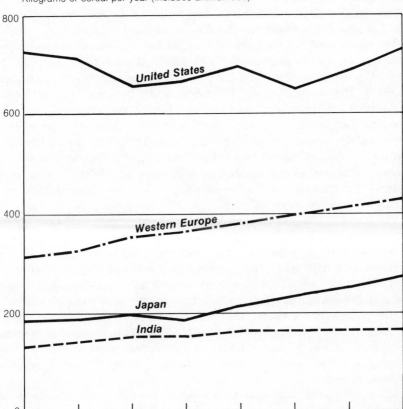

Figure III-2. Per Capita Cereal Consumption

States. In view of the fact that cereal demands in the rich countries already represent a substantial proportion of the total world demand, it is important that we attempt to estimate the future demands for cereals on the part of the rich countries, viewed in terms of growing affluence and changing food technologies.

The poor nations are characterized by high death rates and by high birthrates. For the most part, birthrates hover around 40 to 50 births per 1,000 persons per year, although a few areas have experienced substantial reductions in recent years (e.g., Taiwan, South Korea, Singapore, Hong Kong). Death rates are highly variable, ranging from about 5 per 1,000 (Taiwan, Singapore, Hong Kong) to highs of 25 to 30 in large parts of tropical Africa. There is thus considerable variation in the annual rate of population growth, ranging from a high of 3.4 percent per year (Morocco, Rhodesia, Iraq, Colombia, Ecuador, Venezuela) to a low of about 1.5 percent per year (Jamaica, Argentina, Uruguay).

The vast majority of the inhabitants of developing countries live within the framework of peasant-village culture. Although most persons live on or close to the land, growing their own food, the proportion of persons living in the cities is increasing. The rapid growth of cities in most of the poor countries stems from a combination of rapid population growth, limited availability of land and increasing farm productivity—all coupled with the lure of jobs and money. Unfortunately, however, people are migrating to the cities more rapidly than jobs can be created, or for that matter, more rapidly than services such as housing, water, and sewage can be provided. Large parts of the huge cities of India, such as Calcutta and Bombay, have become vast slums, disease ridden and teeming with hungry unemployed.

The future of the poor nations depends in large measure upon how rapidly population growth can be slowed, agriculture can be modernized, and industries can be created (both in the urban and rural areas). Although fertility rates have decreased in certain areas, quite possibly as a result of the introduction of substantial family planning programs, it is nevertheless possible that the poor countries collectively have not yet reached their peak rate of population growth. Further, there is as yet no clear indication that the rate of population growth in the poor countries will be lowered soon by conscious human action. It seems more likely at present that the rate of growth will lessen as the result of increased mortality stemming from malnutrition brought about by massive shortages of food.

The poor countries have always been highly vulnerable to fluctuations in the availability of cereals. Countless famines have been recorded throughout history and the numbers of persons who have starved to death have increased as the level of human population has grown and as the pressures upon the land have increased. It has been estimated that some two million persons starved to death in the seventeenth century, ten million in the eighteenth century, and twenty-five million in the nineteenth century. Thus far in the twentieth century, which is now three-quarters behind us, about twelve million persons appear to have starved to death, a figure which clearly would be much higher were it not for improved communication and transportation facilities, improved agricultural technology, and the fantastically high agricultural production of North America.

A far more serious problem than famine, at present, is chronic malnutrition. The total number of seriously malnourished people in the world today may be as great as 400 million, or about 16 percent of the population of the poor countries. The effects are reflected in high infant and child mortality rates, perhaps a lasting effect on mental development and learning capacity, a decrease in work output and exacerbation of the effects of parasitic and infectious disease.

World grain production now totals more than 1,200 million tons each year, two-thirds of which is consumed by the affluent countries and one-third by the poor ones. By the year 2020, assuming present trends in population, assuming that the per capita consumption of cereals in the rich countries levels off at the present U.S. level, and assuming *no further increase in the per capita cereal consumption in the poor countries*, total world demand would be over 3,000 million tons, or about 2.5 times the present demand. Were the entire world population in 2020 to be fed at the present U.S. level, demand would be close to 9,000 million tons or 7.5 times the present.

We must ask whether such levels of production are realistically attainable. If they are not, we must ask what steps might realistically be taken to lessen the possibility of a major world disaster.

The Present Situation

In part as a result of the high ratio of arable land to population, but largely because of the intensive application of science and technology to agricultural production, the United States and Canada have emerged as the major suppliers of cereals to the rest of the world. About 85 percent of the North American production is concentrated in the United States. The exports of Australia, the only other net exporter of importance, are only one-fifth of North America's. Altogether, the North American continent accounts for about 20 percent of the world cereal production and of this, about one-third enters world trade. Net world trade in cereals amounts to somewhat less than 8 percent of world production. Most major regions of the world are now net importers of cereals, in part as a result of the fact that affluence has grown more rapidly than agricultural production in most of the rich countries and population has grown so very rapidly in most of the poor ones.

The demands which have been placed upon surplus North American cereal production have fluctuated from year to year and have depended in part upon the harvests in the importing countries and in part upon the financial terms exporters and importers are willing to agree upon. Since 1954, U.S. agricultural production has been so high, relative to demand, that requests of cash purchases could be met and, in addition, substantial shipments of foodstuffs could be made to poor countries under Public Law 480 which permits payment to be made in local noncovertible currency. In addition, the U.S. government has for many years paid its farmers substantial sums of money to keep some fifty million acres of reasonably good farmland idle.

World grain reserves are usually measured in terms of the quantities actually stored at the beginning of a new harvest. During the past fifteen years, these have varied from a high of 155 million metric tons to a low of about 100 million tons or some 8 percent of the annual world production. When reserves are at the lower level, pressures for price increases are substantial.

In recent years, a convergence of trends has resulted in pressures both to draw down stored reserves and to place idled cropland back into production. In addition to the twin pressures of growing affluence and growing population, plant diseases and adverse weather conditions have taken their toll in crop yields in various parts of the world. In the late 1960s, the United States started to bring its idle acres back into production. By 1974, no government payments were made for keeping cropland idle. In the same year, reserve stocks of grain dropped to 90 million tons, a dangerously low level, particularly when we consider that there is no longer any reserve cropland which can easily be put back into production.

As reserves have decreased and demands have increased, food prices have soared. Increased prices have seriously limited the ability of the poor countries to buy needed food. At the same time, food aid to the poor countries has been drastically curtailed. Between 1972 and 1974, wheat shipments under Public Law 480 were decreased by a factor of 4.6 and corn shipments were curtailed by a factor of 2.7.

In late 1973, the member states of the Organization of Petroleum Exporting Countries (OPEC) arbitrarily and suddenly increased the price of crude oil some fourfold—a step which has had dramatic impact upon the world agricultural picture. Over the decades agriculture in the rich nations has become markedly energy dependent and more specifically, petroleum dependent. Most nitrogen fertilizers are produced from oil and natural gas. Numerous pesticides are derived from petrochemicals. Petroleum is needed to run pumps and to power tractors and combines. It is not surprising then that food prices increased rapidly following the increase in the price of crude oil. The price of wheat, for example, jumped quickly from $2 to over $5 per bushel.

In certain of the poor countries, such as India, which are dependent upon petroleum imports, the sudden increase of petroleum prices effectively aborted the so-called Green Revolution, which basically involves the use of plant varieties which can make use of large applications of chemical fertilizers and water. India must import petroleum to run her water pumps and to manufacture fertilizers. Because her nitrogen-fixation capacity is inadequate, she must also import fertilizers, primarily from Japan; because her food production is inadequate, she must also import cereals. All of this has placed enormous strains upon her balance of payments. And even if she were able to afford to purchase all of the fertilizer she needed, she would have had difficulty obtaining it at any price. In May 1974, for example, Japan announced her decision to decrease fertilizer exports to India and China by 15 percent.

Most rich nations are heavy importers of raw materials other than petroleum, primarily from the developing countries. Morocco and Tunisia export phosphates; Bolivia and Malaysia export tin; Jamaica exports bauxite; Peru, Chile, and Zaïre export copper. Following the joint action of the OPEC nations increasing the price of crude oil, Morocco unilaterally quadrupled the export price of phosphate rock, which is essential for the production of phosphate fertilizers. Other phosphate rock suppliers quickly followed suit and shortly thereafter Jamaica increased the export price of bauxite. It now seems likely that export prices of a number of nonrenewable raw materials are destined to increase considerably in the years ahead.

Altogether, about twenty developing countries, inhabited by some 450 million persons, are benefiting or will soon benefit from significant exports of nonrenewable raw materials, including petroleum. Clearly, the money obtained from the sale of these resources, if invested wisely, can accelerate development and can help to alleviate local food shortages.

An additional 900 million persons in the developing world live in countries which are reasonably self-sufficient with respect to nonrenewable resources, including energy. These nations, which include China, Colombia, Mexico, and Peru, for example, were not appreciably harmed by the sudden increase in the price of crude oil.

Another 60 million persons live in countries including South Korea, Taiwan, Hong Kong and Singapore which, like Japan, are closely integrated with the world economy almost entirely through the manufacture of goods.

However, about 925 million people inhabit about forty poor countries which are in serious trouble with respect to raw materials and particularly energy. These include the entire Indian subcontinent, the Philippines, and Egypt. These nations require fertilizers if they are to increase food production and they require energy if they are to increase fertilizer production.

These countries, which are now collectively referred to as "the Fourth World," are the poorest countries in the world and prospects for future economic growth are dismal. They must now pay about $3 billion more each year for essential imports of petroleum fertilizers and food than they were paying previously—and this is money which they do not have. The combined trade deficits of the non-oil developing countries jumped from $9 billion in 1973 to $27 billion in 1974 and to an estimated $36 billion in 1975. Their situation has been exacerbated by the slowdown in the economies of the industrial nations, which is leading to reduced economic assistance, reduced direct private investment, and reduced export earnings.

The countries of the Fourth World are particularly vulnerable to fluctuations in crop yields brought about by the vagaries of weather. Indian agricultural production was severely set back by a drought in 1972/73 and despite a favorable monsoon in 1973, the food situation in 1974 and 1975 remained extremely tight. The most severe famine to strike the Indian subcontinent in three decades took place in Bangladesh, where much of the 1974 summer crop was destroyed by floods. About 50,000 persons died directly of starvation. Many more must have died of related diseases. The region of Africa immediately south of the Sahara known as the Sahelian Zone, stretching from Senegal in the west to northern Ethiopia in the east, suffered from severe drought for five consecutive years, which led to widespread starvation.

It is not difficult to imagine a series of circumstances which could spell disaster for the Fourth World. Were the USSR and China simultaneously to suffer a bad year, as in recent years, they would probably purchase North American grain, paying with convertible currency. Were the monsoons to fail in the Indian subcontinent during the same year and were this to coincide with a drought in the United States, the prospects for the subcontinent would be dismal. The North American cereal available for export would undoubtedly flow to the nations able and willing to pay high prices in convertible currency, rather than to the nations which are unable to pay either now or in the foreseeable future.

The poor countries of the world will undoubtedly be affected in many ways by the fact that oil revenues to the member governments of OPEC increased from $15 billion in 1972 to $43 billion in 1973 to about $133 billion in 1974. As only a fraction of this huge sum can be effectively spent by the OPEC nations themselves, internationally and domestically, a great deal of money remains to be invested elsewhere—most of it in a handful of industrial countries. By 1980, the cumulative surplus is variously estimated to be between $180 and $450 billion (in constant dollars). The Iranians have already bought a controlling interest in the great German firm, Krupp. Much of the revenues are placed in banks in industrial countries on short-term deposit. Much of the revenues are spent on military equipment. Although there is much talk of OPEC nations helping the less fortunate developing countries, thus far there are few signs of truly substantial action. The Oil Facility of the International Monetary Fund has provided loans which have covered some 40 percent of the oil import bills of developing countries. Regional banks, such as the Asian Development Bank, are increasing their loans to help overcome the impact of higher oil prices.

Most of the oil importing industrial countries, on the other hand, are suffering from serious balance-of-payment problems, in no small measure magnified by the rise in the price of crude oil. In 1974, the annual British trade deficit alone was about $9 billion and the combined deficits of the industrial countries was $67 billion. The combination of these two related circumstances obviously gives the OPEC nations unprecedented financial and political power. So vast is this problem that our traditional financial and international political institutions have difficulty coping with the situation on a global basis.

These circumstances are having profound effect upon the relationships between the rich countries and the poor ones. So severe are the problems of the industrial countries that those of the less developed countries tend to get pushed under the table. Indeed, present U.S. policy seems to be to downgrade both capital and technical assistance. The ultimate consequences of these changing attitudes can at present be only dimly perceived. They are, nevertheless, awesome to contemplate.

Problems of Increasing the Availability of Food

There is little, if any, potential for increasing the area of farmland in the most populous areas of the developing world. However, considerable increases in food production could be obtained in those areas by increasing crop yields. This would necessitate the modernization of agriculture, by which is meant applying the results of modern science and technology to growing, protecting, harvesting, storing, transporting, and distributing agricultural products. It also means the development of the social and economic institutions which make possible the effective application of modern agricultural technology.

The so-called Green Revolution has been based upon the fact that it is possible to select and cultivate genetic varieties of plants which can thrive in local environmental conditions and which can effectively utilize high concentrations of fertilizers, given adequate quantities of water. In India, substantial areas were set aside for the purpose of growing new high-yielding varieties of wheat. Tube wells were drilled which, in many cases, provided ample water for two or three crops per year. Grain production per hectare increased enormously—until the discontinuity appeared which was created by the sudden increase in petroleum prices. More often than not, water pumps are powered by diesel oil. Most nitrogenous fertilizers are produced from petroleum or natural gas. Not long after the OPEC countries increased the price of crude oil, exporters of phosphate rock increased their prices substantially.

There is little question that crop yields in much of the developing world can be increased considerably. However, this involves a multiplicity of developments, some of which are:

1. Breeding of plant species which can grow satisfactorily in the local environment;
2. Provision of adequate quantities of fertilizer;
3. Provision of adequate quantities of water;
4. Provision of adequate quantities of pesticides.

In addition, farmers must be persuaded to use the new techniques and shown how to use them. All of this takes a great deal of time and a great deal of money, coupled with planning and organization on a large scale. Most of the Fourth World countries are simply unable to mobilize the necessary funds and organization without outside help.

There are areas of the developing world which could, in principle, make possible a sizable increase in the world's agricultural lands. These areas lie primarily in the hot, humid tropics where the soils are primarily lateritic. Unfortunately, we do not yet know how to manage such soils successfully. A great deal of research and development will be necessary before this can be accomplished. In principle, large wet tropical areas could be developed for fish culture or for growing water plants which, in turn, could be fed to livestock. But again, a great deal of research and money would be required. There are also large arid areas in the developing world which could be cultivated were there adequate supplies of water. In such situations the engineering requirements and the monetary and energy costs are vast. Again, a great deal of outside help would be required.

No matter how we view the situation, enormous efforts will be required if the poor countries are to become self-sufficient in the production of foodstuffs. All approaches to accomplishing this should be explored, but for the moment, the most rapid and least costly approach would appear to be to concentrate a major effort aimed at modernizing agriculture.

With respect to the rich countries, there is little potential for new farmlands in Europe or Japan. Even the Soviet Union has little potential for increasing the size of its cultivated lands significantly. Indeed, in some parts of the rich world, the area of cultivated land has actually been decreasing as the result of the encroachment of cities, industries, airports, and highways upon what had been good agricultural land. Further, in many areas of the world, both rich and poor, much agricultural land is lost each year because of processes of erosion which result from bad land management.

A considerable increase in agricultural production is possible in the USSR as she improves her agricultural productivity through more effective organization and research. Improvements in yields in both Eastern and Western Europe can also be anticipated. But the greatest potential for increases in agricultural production in the rich countries lies in the present exporting countries—and particularly in North America and Australia. With sufficient capital investment, according to the U.S. Department of Agriculture, the harvested acreage in the United States could be expanded from the present 318 million acres to about 350 million acres by 1985. Further, an additional 200 million acres now used as pasture, range, and forest are potentially cultivatable. However, we must keep in mind that the best lands are already in use. Much of the potentially cultivatable acreage is in the arid western states where the soil is of marginal fertility. Large inputs of irrigation water, fertilizers, and pesticides would be required and the environmental effects might be substantial. As a result, experts suggest that this currently uncropped land be brought into production using great caution.

Considerable improvements in crop yields are also possible in the United States. The Department of Agriculture estimates that by 1985 corn harvests could be increased by 57 percent, soybean harvests could rise 44 percent, wheat 35 percent, and feed grains 50 percent. This would require, however, the application of greatly increased quantities of irrigation water, fertilizers, and pesticides. Here, again, the environmental effects could be substantial.

We cannot expect any substantial increase in the harvest of fish from the sea, which on a worldwide basis is comparable in importance to beef in the human diet. Since World War II fishing technology has become so efficient that we may already be harvesting the maximum quantity possible on a steady-state basis. Indeed there is good evidence that some species such as halibut and haddock have been overharvested.

It must be emphasized that one critical element of world agricultural production is almost completely out of man's control—and that is weather. Within any decade there are irregularities in rainfall patterns, some of which can inflict enormous damage to crops. In 1973, Bangladesh suffered the results of catastrophic floods. In recent years, the region south of the Sahara Desert suffered from several consecutive years of drought. The major U.S. corn and wheat areas suffer from what appear to be periodic droughts—one struck in 1974, adding to the seriousness of the shortage of cereals in the world. Occasionally, adverse conditions appear in a number of major areas simultaneously, as in 1972 when bad seasons in China and the USSR combined with widespread corn blight in the United States to produce a serious world shortage which placed an enormous drain upon world reserves.

In addition to such aberrations, there are long-term climatic trends which are not well understood but which can profoundly affect the world agricultural picture. Both the long-term geological and the short-term historical records show that there have been enormous climatic changes in the past. There will undoubtedly be similar substantial climatic changes in the future and, indeed, we may well be enmeshed in a major global change at the present time.

Weather records indicate strongly that, beginning at the turn of the century, the Northern Hemisphere began to warm and temperatures rose to levels higher than at any time in the past millennium. The temperature peaked about 1940, has been falling rapidly since that time and may well soon reach at least the colder levels which prevailed prior to the turn of the century. Were this to happen, growing seasons in the Northern Hemisphere would become shorter and rainfall patterns would shift. Such a development could have profound effect upon the world agricultural picture.

Prior to the emergence of humanity as a major geological and ecological force, climatic changes had resulted from the complex interactions of a multiplicity of natural phenomena. Since we appeared upon the earth scene, a new force has been added to the climatic picture which is probably substantial but by no means clearly understood. We know that (our) various activities should affect climate in various ways, but it is extremely difficult to put the effects on a quantitative basis. Clearly deforestation and overgrazing have had impact in the past. With industrialization, the addition of increasing quantities of particulate matter, carbon dioxide, and heat to the atmosphere are having their effects today and will have an even greater effect in the future. The results need not necessarily be adverse, but they might well be.

**Problems of Decreasing the Rates of Growth of
Population and Affluence**

It is clear that at some time the growth of both population and affluence must
stop. It remains to be seen just how this will happen—both are difficult to
influence. Birth control pills enable us to slow down the growth of population to
a certain extent in some cultures. Unfortunately, there is no such thing as an
affluence control pill which is effective in any culture.

Since World War II, a number of countries have established policies which are
aimed at limiting the size of families. Some of these programs have been
effective; others have had little effect. The fact remains that birthrates must be
greatly reduced if in the long run the food-population problem is to be resolved.

On a time scale of one or two years the question as to whether or not a poor
country has a population policy is unimportant. But a growth rate of 2.5 percent
per year means that in ten years there will be nearly 30 percent more people to
feed and that in a quarter century there will be nearly twice the present number.
In the long run, population policies are essential.

By 1970, about twenty-five countries, embracing more than two-thirds of the
population of the poor countries, had established population policies and family
planning programs. Another fifteen countries, embracing some 12 percent of the
population of the poor countries, were providing family planning support in the
absence of an official governmental policy. Thus, in varying degrees, governments which embrace nearly 90 percent of the population of the poor countries
support family planning programs. This does not mean, however, that their
support is necessarily effective.

An affirmative national population policy is clearly an important element of
success. Beyond that, there must be adequate birth control technology, motivation among the people to accept family planning, and national organization
which can implement the policy. Unfortunately there are few nations in which
all of these conditions exist.

With respect to birth control technology, many advances have been made in
recent years. We have the contraceptive pill, the intrauterine device, and
improved methods of sterilization and abortion. Accelerated research and
development programs are likely to give us improved technologies, including
effective chemical abortifacients and a "once-a-month" pill. Unfortunately,
however, little has been done to link birth control technologies to cultural
preferences.

With respect to organization there have been serious problems, even in
situations where the national will is strong. Many countries with favorable
policies do not in fact have significant programs. Lip service with respect to
family planning more often than not exceeds concrete action. Most alarming is
the fact that certain of the poor countries with large populations, including the
entire Indian subcontinent, do not have at present reasonable organizational
capacities for family planning programs.

The problem of personal motivation to limit births appears to be by far the most serious one. Although peasants in most cultures are interested in preventing births, the motivations are not high considering the technological means available for limiting births. Indeed, there are substantial traditional cultural factors which work against the establishment of effective family planning programs.

Although there are some favorable signs, the overall prognosis with respect to population growth in the world is gloomy. Clearly, many things can be done, but for the most part they are not being done.

With respect to the growth of affluence, the petroleum exporting nations have come close to inventing an "affluence control pill." By increasing the price of crude oil by a factor of four, they appreciably slowed economic growth in many industrial countries. But this forced measure is inadequate from many points of view. In the long run, the rich countries must ask themselves many searching questions. How rich do they want to be? How rich *need* they be for their people to lead rewarding lives, free of poverty and deprivation?

For many years the Soviet Union has suggested, and this concept has been echoed by many of the poor countries, that population growth is a phenomenon of secondary importance—that were economic development to take place sufficiently rapidly, the population problem would take care of itself. Those who hold this view point to the decrease in birthrates in the industrialized world during the nineteenth and twentieth centuries and suggest that as development takes place in the years ahead the rate of population growth will slacken. This view was expressed strongly at the 1974 Population Conference in Bucharest. But the world of 1974 is quite unlike that of the world of 1874. It is inconceivable that the heavily populated poor countries of today can even remotely go through the transition which was experienced decades ago by those countries which are now rich. The conditions are in no way comparable.

In any event, an essential element of the evolution of U.S. policy concerning food involves a willingness to stress that population growth and the growth of affluence are critical elements of our future.

Ameliorative Measures

As we attempt to formulate possible U.S. policies, it is important that we recognize that the food-population problem is itself a vast system composed of a large number of interrelated parts. Once we understand this, we can appreciate that there is no such thing as a "solution" to the overall problem. Rather, if the broad problem is to be brought under control, the resolution of a number of component problems must be pursued simultaneously. Many choices and combinations of choices are possible.

At one extreme, for example, the United States might elect to try to provide, on a continuing basis, adequate supplies of food with "no strings attached" to the Fourth World to avoid nutritional disaster. At the other extreme, the United States might elect to ignore the Fourth World—to cease selling grain on concessional terms and limit sales to ones which are paid for in cash with convertible currency. Both extremes seem to this author to be unrealistic from the points of view of both practicality and morality. A number of alternative possibilities must be thoroughly explored.

We must keep in mind that the problems which confront us are on three quite different time scales:

1. The immediate problem of using existing agricultural production and reserves in such a way as to minimize the human suffering in the Fourth World and to avoid disaster before the next harvest (time scale less than one year);
2. The long-range problem of securing regional self-sufficiency (time scale of one hundred years);
3. The intermediate problem of expanding and utilizing effectively the food surpluses of the rich exporting nations in such a way that the needs of both rich and poor importing nations can be reasonably met during the transition period (time scale of twenty-five years).

A resolution of the world food-population problem clearly would involve in varying degrees the following very broad long-range interrelated goals:

1. Increasing world food production in such a way that each major area of the world becomes self-sufficient;
2. Increasing the efficiency of food utilization and distribution;
3. Decreasing the rate of growth of affluence;
4. Decreasing the rate of growth of population;
5. Establishing a carefully controlled international food reservoir which can be drawn upon in years of poor crop yields and replenished during years of relative abundance;
6. Establishing an efficient world system for estimating harvests in all regions of the world in time to make the necessary adjustments in world cereal distribution.

As an illustration of ways in which a common acceptance of such a set of goals might be effective in ameliorating the present difficulties, let us imagine that a group of nations, both rich and poor, were to create an international agency for cereal distribution. All nations which subscribe to the six basic goals enumerated above would be eligible for membership. Member states would agree to deal only with the agency in the sale and purchase of cereals.

The Cereal Agency would maintain a grain reservoir which would be built up and maintained at an average level of perhaps 200 million tons (about a two-month world supply). The agency would make purchases from cereal exporting nations at locally competitive prices, handled in such a way that the reserve would normally fall no lower than 150 million tons and rise no higher than 250 million tons.

The agency would sell grain to rich importing nations at about the purchase price, but adjusted to take into account ability to pay (per capita GNP). Grain would be sold to poor countries at substantially reduced prices which would be related to per capita GNP, but which would also be related to birthrate. No nation would be permitted to purchase in a given year more than a certain limit which might be set at something like 150 kilograms per person, representing approximately Japan's current per capita import requirements. Nations which export cereals (e.g., the People's Republic of China) would be ineligible to purchase cereals at reduced prices until imports exceed exports. No nation would be permitted to export cereals which are imported from the agency.

All member states would pay dues which would be used, in part, to defray the operating cost of the system, to pay for agricultural technical assistance as well as to help defray the costs of selling grain to poor countries at substantially reduced prices. Basically a nation's dues might be proportional to its GNP, but with builtin incentives aimed at decreasing the growth of both affluence and population. For example, dues might also be made proportional to both the per capita GNP and the birthrate.

As an illustration of how such a system might work from a quantitative point of view, it is instructive to apply some numbers. Figure III-3 shows the flow of cereals in the world in 1972. Table III-3 gives a breakdown of the percentages of imports or exports involving specific regions or countries.

Were a system such as is described above in operation today, cereal costs and dues might be somewhat as is shown in Table III-4, assuming for the purpose of discussion, that basic payments by the agency to the exporting countries for cereals would be about $200 per ton.

Given such a system we can optimistically imagine a series of developments which could relieve the world food situation significantly by the turn of the century.

With respect to increasing production in the exporting countries, an annual increase of 2.5 percent might be achieved with effort by 1980 and 3.5 percent by the year 2000. Increasing production in the importing rich countries would be considerably more difficult, but an annual increase of about one percent might be maintained. Potential increases in production in the poor countries are substantial and might be raised from 2.5 percent per year to about 3.5 percent per year by the turn of the century. Under such assumptions something like the production levels shown in Table III-5 would appear plausible.

Levels of demand will depend, of course, upon levels of population. If we are optimistic and assume that the rate of population growth of the rich countries will continue to fall and that the rate of growth of the poor countries falls from 2.5 percent per year to 1.5 percent per year by the turn of the century, the poor

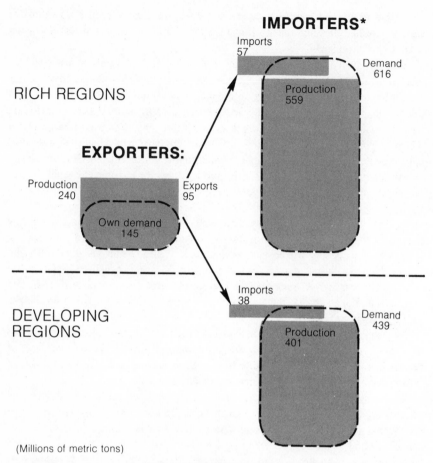

(Millions of metric tons)

*Includes those countries classed as "intermediate" in Section 1.

Figure III-3. Flow of Cereals, 1972

countries could become self-sufficient in cereals at a level of 200 kg. per person by the year 2000, while the per capita consumption in the rich countries could be held at a level of about 700 kg. per year.

Something like two billion dollars each year would be made available by the agency for technical assistance efforts in the poor countries. Such efforts should be concentrated on:

1. Projects aimed at increasing agricultural productivity in the poor countries;
2. Projects aimed at increasing the efficiency of food utilization and distribution;

Table III-3
Exporters and Importers of Cereals (1972)
(expressed in terms of percentages of flows in U.S. dollars)

Country or Region	Percentage
Exporting Regions	
United States	61.9
Canada	21.9
Australia	12.9
South Africa	3.3
Importing Regions	
Western Europe (including Greece, Israel and New Zealand)	25.0
Japan	16.3
Eastern Europe	10.0
USSR	8.5
Total rich countries	59.8
Poorest developing countries	9.0
OPEC countries	10.0
Other developing countries	21.1
Total developing countries	40.0

3. Establishment of an efficient world system for estimating and monitoring harvests;
4. Assistance in the development of national population policies and family planning programs;
5. Development of research programs in all of these areas.

The agency would be free to make use of existing international mechanisms for channeling funds or to make direct grants, whichever would be most effective.

The activities of the agency would be in addition to the activities of the existing international organizations, including the funding agencies, and hopefully would be supplemented by a variety of bilateral technical assistance programs. In this connection, the United States might well decide to reorient and reorganize its entire foreign assistance program in such a way that:

1. All capital assistance is channeled through international institutions; and,
2. A new national institution is established specifically designed for rendering effective technical assistance and expediting technological transfer.

In many situations technical assistance can be more effectively given bilaterally than through international agencies. Experience has shown, however, that

Table III-4
Hypothetical Flows of Money Through International Cereal Agency*

Rich countries export 95 million tons @ $200/ton	$ 19.0 billion
Operating costs (including agricultural technical assistance) @ 10%	1.9
Total cost	$ 20.9 billion
Rich importing countries purchase 57 million tons @ $200/ton	$ 11.4 billion
Poor importing countries purchase 38 million tons @ $50/ton	1.9
Total return	$ 13.3 billion
Deficit to be made up from dues	$ 7.6 billion
Dues for rich countries (average 0.29% of GNP)	$ 7.34 billion
Dues for poor countries (average 0.063% of GNP)	0.26
Return from U.S. cereal exports @ $200/ton	$ 11.76 billion
U.S. dues	2.33
Net return to U.S.	$ 9.43 billion
Net return per ton of cereal exports by U.S.	$160.00
Total costs of cereals to rich importing countries @ $200/ton	$ 11.4 billion
Dues of rich importing countries	4.3
Total cost to rich importing countries	$ 15.7 billion
Net cost to rich importing countries per ton of imported cereal	$275.00
Net cost to poor importing countries per ton of imported cereal	$ 57.00

*Assuming 1972 Flow of Cereals and Average Payment to Exporters of $200 per Metric Ton (1972 Dollars)

Table III-5
Possible Future Cereal Production Levels
(millions of metric tons)

Year	Rich Exporters	Rich Importers	Poor	World Total
1972	240	560	400	1,200
1980	290	620	520	1,430
1990	380	680	700	1,760
2000	510	750	990	2,250

bilateral technical assistance programs must be planned very carefully if they are to be effective and that both the planning and implementation stages must be completely cooperative. Given the wide range of national and human endowments, investments, government policies and needs, methods and strategies for technology transfer must be tailored to an individual country's national development goals.

A recent study suggests the creation of a United States-based public foundation, created by the Congress, supported principally from public funds with multiple-year authorization and congressional oversight.[a] The foundation would facilitate access to U.S. scientific and technological activities in U.S. government laboratories, universities, research institutes, and the private sector. Counterpart binational foundations or commissions would be created in individual countries which choose to participate. Guided by the development goals of the country, the local groups would have flexibility and funds to seek assistance over the broad range of activities in which science and technology have a role, including agriculture and family planning.

An important aspect of the binational foundation concept is that of joint funding. In all cases costs would be shared, thus removing the program from the donor-client relationship. The proportion of national funding would be varied from one country to another, perhaps using a formula based upon per capita GNP.

Finally, it is important for us to reexamine the roles of private U.S.-based organizations with respect to the world food-population problem. The major organizations which place substantial efforts in the area include the Population Council, the Agricultural Development Council, the Overseas Development Council, and Resources for the Future. In recent years all of these organizations have developed programs of high quality and of considerable effectiveness.

In view of the fact that it is impossible to divorce the problems of food, population, and development from each other, it would appear that these organizations could profit from working more closely together, coordinating their programs and sharing tasks. Indeed, it seems to this author that the three councils might conceivably merge to create a new balanced private organization prepared to examine the problems of development in their totality and in which no one aspect of the development problem would be disproportionately visible.

---

[a]National Academy of Sciences, The International Development Institute, Board on Science and Technology for International Development, Washington, July, 1971.

IV
Some Solutions to the Food Problem

James L. Draper and Jon R. Elam

Causes and Effects

World food needs could be met, at least into the twenty-first century, with techniques and resources which are now at hand. The interrelated caveats surrounding such a statement may be categorized as: (1) technological, (2) political, and (3) cultural.

Available information in technical agricultural literature leaves little doubt that food production sufficient in both amount and content to meet world population needs is possible, even with drastic curtailment of fossil fuel energy for the mechanized sectors of the production/processing/marketing complex. Adequate output is dependent on decentralization of production into smaller units which everywhere prove themselves more efficient in utilization of land, water, and fossil fuel energy.

Commitment to the changes necessary to effect economies of land, water, and fossil energy use is doubtful under present national and international conditions, however, and may not occur until the starvation of some millions of human beings in Asia and Africa penetrates the consciousness of the developed nations. Preoccupation with possession of wealth in the form of fossil fuel resources, food stores, and weapons obscures more pressing problems, and it may be that cataclysmic international events will have to occur before the substantial changes which are necessary in food production and delivery can come about.

The purpose here is to cite what seem, on the basis of available information,

97

to be logical technological alterations, rather than to analyze the political, cultural, and economic forces which must interact to bring them about. Full utilization of the four elements of food production—land, water, solar energy, and genetic resources—has not been approached, except on small farm units. Furthermore, efficiencies in tillage, irrigation, pest control, harvesting, and storage have been demonstrated as feasible and capable of around 10 percent.

Dissemination of information on simple improvements in cultural practices can, as has been amply demonstrated, be accomplished far better by use of paraprofessionals than by the use of professionals who are more attuned to the techniques of larger production units. In addition, in several states, extension of credit to small full-time or part-time energy-efficient farmers has helped them double their gross output and more than double their labor income. Credit in small amounts is more troublesome to administer, but that is beside the point. Success of efforts during the depression days demonstrates that it can be accomplished.

Of the $132 billion paid for food in the United States in 1973, only $50 billion reached the hard-pressed producer. This illustrates the absurdity of the capital-intensive, labor-extensive system, which is now being exported on the same ships which transport American agricultural machinery, and multinational corporate involvement to nations which still have land capable of being exploited in the same way that large alluvial plains in the United States are being exploited today by mechanized farming. The British economist E.F. Schumacher, during a recent series of lectures in the United States, mentioned that wheat from Kansas was being processed near Seattle, Washington, into low-quality breakfast food to be sold in Boston supermarkets. How much better it would have been, he noted, to utilize whole grain wheat or whole-wheat flour near to where it is produced, which is in virtually all of the contiguous forty-eight states.

A 1967 U.S. Department of Agriculture study of American farm size indicated that no matter what the specifics are from a human development standpoint, the more people taking part in decisions, the healthier the climate for production, economic growth, and development. Experience in Midwestern states, which have a long and stubborn tradition of family-sized farms, indicates much higher yields in terms of fossil energy expenditures, and more community participation in economic and political decisions than in the large farm areas of California and the Southern Delta states. Similar phenomena are noted in India, where per hectare yields on the average farm (less than 5 acres) are nearly 50 percent higher than on farms of more than 50 acres. In Taiwan, where small farmers have clear access to needed inputs of capital, technical assistance, and cooperative marketing techniques, farms of less than 2-1/2 acres have far higher per acre yields than do those of more than 5 acres.

Where small-scale mechanization and intermediate technology (e.g., seed drills, rotary tillers, and small, portable irrigation pumps) are used to supplement rather than supplant human efforts, productivity of the land and conservation of the topsoil increases, whether it is in the United States or any other country.

The myth that one American farmer can feed fifty other people is not true and never has been true. The fact is that what used to be farm labor has been moved to towns and cities, into establishments which process, distribute, and sell food; every dollar of wages and interest, all the profits which implement manufacturers make—all are part of the farm labor dollar, now paid by corporations in cities and towns rather than being received by the farmer and dispensed by him. The largest and most conservative farm organization in California, the Farm Bureau Federation, recently asserted that one-third of the state's employment is in agriculture or agriculture-related industries.

Significantly, however, it is not California's farmers who have control of any segment of the production/processing/marketing complex, since that state's farm production, which is the largest in the nation, is dominated by corporate entities domiciled outside the state and with few state controls over their activities. Basic environmental regulations of those corporations' actions are subject to almost constant and largely ineffectual complaints by citizen groups which charge inadequacies in both the regulations and their enforcement.

Per capita consumption of paper in the United States, at its present annual rate of more than 750 pounds (ten times Europe's consumption) and projected to be 1,000 pounds by the turn of the century, is another significant contributor to the land monopoly situation and to the shortage and high price (an increase of 35 percent has been recorded in six years) of rowcrop land available in the United States. Increasingly—in Wisconsin, Maine, Georgia, Florida, Alabama, Mississippi, Arkansas, and many other states—paper and timber companies, which have intertwined directorates and close-friend management among themselves and with other institutions, buy up every sizable tract available. Tree farming, which paper manufacturers hail as the "saving trend of the industry," has been instituted on many thousands of acres of former pasture and cropland. Tree farming, which requires about one-tenth of the manpower of even mechanized cotton production, in many countries is *increasing* the flow of unprepared thousands of rural people into cities, which are equally unprepared to receive and house and employ them. Thus, in addition to removing thousands of acres from crop and pasture totals, American paper consumption habits and the companies which exploit them add to urban blight and ghetto unrest.

American cattle producers, who have strong political voices and close linkages with America's corporate giants, are fond of proclaiming that they use for grazing land which otherwise would be wasted. But this obscures the fact that fully 40 percent of the pasture land in this country could be planted in crops and that in fact much of it once was in crops. Cattlemen are able to use cropland for pasture largely because they are able to employ accelerated depreciation schedules for their breeding stock. This enables them to hold land for speculation. They know it is appreciating in value at about 6 percent annually and that they will pay no taxes on this unearned increment until the time of selling the land, and then on a capital gains basis.

Agriculture no longer has national boundaries. Increasingly, multinational corporations involved in farming and farm-related business are dependent on production and processing outside the United States, and on selling in American supermarkets. This enables them to shift costs internationally and from subsidiary to subsidiary to meet tax avoidance needs. Unfortunately, this has the effect of removing local, state, or even national needs and priorities from considerations and emphasizes the profit motive at the expense of human values.

Multinational agriculture thus adds to the litany of absurdities. It obviously is not farmers or their marketing organizations who profit from international sales of grain and other food commodities, but rather international trading corporations. Neither do consumers anywhere benefit directly, but only marginally as users of commodities whose prices are determined by the peculiar genius of the global corporation to organize delivery of goods on a vaster scale than any other institution in the history of mankind.

There is another important and obvious element which cannot be omitted from this indictment of the American-born mechanized agricultural system. This element is the profit-only motivation which is essential in the structure and financial makeup of the phenomenon called the food corporation. Such a motivation forces decisions based on dollar gain rather than on nutritional value of the commodity that is produced. Cosmetic treatment of food results when chemicals are used which produce attractive color rather than improved vitamin and mineral content, when genetic manipulation is used to change size and texture with protein and storability disregarded. These are familiar examples in today's corporate food world.

It may be, however, that in state-trading nations like the USSR, and now the OPEC countries with their solid front on availability and price of oil supplies, there is a countervailing force to the international food cartel. Such a force may not only affect the flow of oil supplies but also show an ability to bargain over corporate profits of American-based firms. What the Shah of Iran refers to as a "recycling of wealth" would help push along the poorest nations without bankrupting the developed countries.

The Short-Term Solution

The energy situation confronts large-scale American agriculture at its most vulnerable point—the dependence on large machinery rather than manpower for performing its tasks.

In the short-term, the needs of mechanized agriculture must be met even at the expense of serious curtailment of other segments of the economy. Fortunately, on-the-farm production consumes only 3 percent of the American supply of energy. This is equal to roughly one-eighth of the energy used in American transportation, and an even smaller portion of the energy used by the manufacturing sector. Short-term needs of farming could be met by a relatively small curtailment of transportation, with nonessential driving of personal automobiles and recreation vehicles being the obvious first choices for immediate reductions.

The seriousness of the situation, in view of the lack of grain reserves, cannot be overemphasized. A failure to address the immediate needs of farmers for energy and fertilizer should be considered irresponsible at its best and ominous at its worst.

Politically, action on this front should not be too difficult. The Congress is ready for resolute action and may well initiate legislation in behalf of food production even without Administration leadership in that direction. A long-term solution, however, although essential if food production/processing is to become less energy-dependent, may prove much more difficult, since it is certain to require a combination of economic, technological, political, and even cultural decisions which will prove unpalatable to broad sectors of the society. Nevertheless, a long-term solution is an absolute essential if there is to be hope of food production keeping pace with worldwide population growth, which now is estimated to be at a rate of slightly less than 2 percent annually.

The only alternative to rather drastic agricultural reforms is implementation of a degree of international economic and political partnership which at this point in man's development is utterly impossible. But even if there were to be a giant leap forward into international amity and cooperation, the effects of such cooperation could be only temporary, since supplies of fossil fuel energy are finite and someday will be exhausted.

The United Nations' Food and Agriculture Organization estimates that there will be 750 million malnourished people in the world if present food production and distribution patterns continue to 1985. This serves to underline the seriousness of the food/political problem, since those 750 million persons, wherever they might be, would constitute one-fifth of the world population, making their hunger a political force of heretofore unimagined potential—either within or without an international body like the United Nations. Hence, the conclusion that changes in agriculture's fossil fuel energy dependence must come is inescapable.

An Interim Necessity: Supply Stability

The U.S. Department of Agriculture policy is symbiotic with an essentially free market situation with respect to agricultural commodities. There is no reserve stock program, no viable production control program, no import/export control—with the result that both the American consumer and the producer find themselves at the cracking end of the whip with respect to domestic farm and food prices. Any major disturbance in the supply situation worldwide has immediate and sharp price repercussions in the U.S. market. A change in supply of about one-half of 1 percent results in a change in price of at least 1 percent. And since the governments of most regular importing countries understand that world population is probably outreaching supply, they make every effort, including paying price premiums, to keep grain flowing into their countries to avoid political repercussions.

What exists now in the world of food and agriculture is a wild scramble for supplies, with sharply erratic prices when total supplies become just a shade short. And in the absence of an adequate storage program and supply management mechanism, marketable supplies of grain in the United States increase or decrease rapidly, and vastly out of proportion to supply-demand situations. So there is still no real effort at agricultural planning in the United States, but it would seem that reasonably firm data exist around which plans could be made.

As Professor Willard Cochrane of the University of Minnesota points out, "If the United States doesn't develop some sort of long-range plan to deal with interrelationships of domestic demand, export demand, and food aid programs, we shall continue to have agricultural economic uncertainty, price and income instability, and terrific political pressure when we continue to follow the present USDA free market policy."

Several proposals for food reserves have been advanced. Most economists feel that substantial emergency stocks would not bring decreases in prices received by farmers if net accumulations were made to reach desired levels over a period of three or four years and if the food products released to developing countries did not displace quantities that would be purchased in commercial markets.

The Council for Agricultural Science and Technology suggests that there should be a system for emergency reserves which would be owned by countries of origin, subject to international agreement on amounts to be accumulated, on distribution of reserves, and on timing of release. Costs for the stockpiles would be borne by the developing nations in agreed-upon degrees. Several ideas for structure are being proposed. One is that nations with finances but not grain surpluses (the Middle East, for example) and those with actual production surpluses (United States, Canada, Argentina, and others) would hold the actual grain within their boundaries but under control of an international body. An FAO proposal suggests that because of transportation problems of the past, one-third to one-half of the storage should be pre-positioned in strategic areas.

There is, to be sure, a considerable information vacuum on nation-by-nation production and cereal stock availability and a serious lack of international information exchange. A reserve program could have a profoundly stabilizing effect on the U.S. grain market in addition to building reserves for use of developing nations. Congress might determine a price range that could vary from month to month, taking, for example, the average of the range for the previous three months as the purchase price goal above which the reserve program would not enter the market. There is ample precedent in attempts at grain stabilization programs in this country, although not all have been successful.

Whatever solutions are tried, it is imperative that they be multinational or nonnational in scope, purpose, and participation. The United States might well take the initiative by pursuing a policy agenda similar to this:

1. Announce to the world its domestic requirements and its trade requirements of regular foreign customers, and indicate that those supply requirements will be protected. This insures a stable demand-supply market at a stable price.
2. Announce requirements monthly, indicate whether they are ahead of or behind demand schedule, and indicate whether it is a situation which may require the use of reserve stocks.
3. Utilize a flexible budget pool (at least $2-3 billion) to support the food aid programs which would be used to purchase stocks, thus guaranteeing the developing countries their fair share of the market. This also would allow for some market flexibility.
4. Sales of grains to state-trading nations like the USSR would be negotiated by the U.S. government with an eye to volume, price, and other economic considerations, such as transportation methods, delivery schedules, etc. Private grain firms would still be responsible for accumulating the orders and handling grain, but would be forced to work within the requirements of (1), (2), and (3) above.
5. The United States could protect its commitments under (1), (2), and (3) by announced export controls.

This type of planning strategy could help the market return to somewhat more tranquility than is evident at present. Since most producers groups would be able to advise their members before planting time, alternative crops could be seeded to avert over planting of crops expected to be in surplus.

If an internationally coordinated emergency reserve policy should come into effect, it could also be influential in dealing with international inflation problems, since the market would be based on commodities rather than on fluctuating currency exchange rates. One such plan is being developed by the International Independence Institute of Ashby, Massachusetts.

Essential Long-Term Changes

Priorities for changes would be difficult to assign, but certainly they should include the following:

1. *Decentralization.* Farming in the United States must move toward labor-intensive, energy/capital-extensive units to replace the present mode. In "primitive cultures" five to fifty food calories can be obtained for each calorie of energy invested. Some highly civilized cultures have done as well and occasionally better. In sharp contrast, industrialized food systems require five to ten

calories of fuel to produce one food calorie. We must pay special attention to this difference.

2. *Tax Reform.* Tax changes must be instituted to remove the advantages of accelerated depreciation now held by capital-intensive operations and to give preference to smaller, family-sized units.

3. *Protein Sources.* The issue of whether the United States should reduce the amount of grain fed to livestock, where it is less efficient in producing food for human beings, presents itself in stark, humanitarian terms.

Feed conversion studies sponsored by the U.S. Senate Select Committee on Nutrition and Human Needs show that on a calorie for calorie and protein for protein basis, it is more efficient for people to consume grains directly (than through livestock). Grain consumed directly by people provides two to ten times the calories it would if converted to livestock products. Furthermore, the protein and other nutrients available in livestock products are not substantially better than those in cereals—it is only necessary to combine different cereals in the same meal to produce the full complement of essential amino acids which comprise complete protein. Finally, 1,000 lbs. of corn converts to 736 lbs. of cornmeal, but to only 275 lbs. of chicken. However, on a dollar to dollar basis, conversion of corn, soy bean meal, and other concentrates to livestock produces several times more valuable foods than would conversion to cornmeal or soy flour.

4. *Farms and Rural Development.* Every effort must be made to get adequate funding for the Rural Development Act, particularly the sections dealing with technical aid to family farm units and development of farm-related infrastructures in community development. Additionally, passage of the Family Farm Act would aid production units less dependent on fossil fuel energy.

5. *Soil and Water Conservation.* Prohibition of the destruction of aquifers in areas dependent on them for home water supplies, irrigation, and downstream water supplies should be as nearly absolute as possible, whether the aquifers are coal seams, impermeable stone, or clay. The "small watershed" concepts of the Soil Conservation Service programs of the 1930s should be revived in order to preserve water where it falls, by means of ponds, terrace systems, and moderate-sized impoundments. Such a program proved it could cut erosion soil losses to the barest minimum.

6. *Land Inventory and Controls.* There should be an immediate program to inventory land resources on a farm-by-farm and county-by-county basis, with ownership maps published for use of county officials and community groups, so that there can be rational and equitable planning for reviving energy-efficient family agriculture. The use of prime agricultural land for any other purpose should be prohibited. Agricultural land is being lost to shopping centers, housing, and highway construction now at a rate of about a million acres annually in the United States.

7. *Solar and Wind Energy.* The United States should embark immediately on

a program to gain maximum utilization of solar and wind energy, employing small-scale, individually and community controlled models already developed in some sections of the Southwest, and embarking on a substantial research and development program in these fields and in utilization of wave pumps.

8. *Production Cooperatives.* There should be legislation establishing, encouraging, and institutionalizing *production* cooperatives which enable farmers to own land in common and to farm it cooperatively. (Legislative and regulatory decisions in the past have permitted loans to supply and marketing cooperatives but have prohibited similar assistance to production cooperatives, thus discouraging an extremely efficient and labor-intensive form of agriculture widely practiced in countries outside the United States.)

9. *Irrigation Limitations.* Litigation should be instituted immediately to obtain U.S. Department of the Interior enforcement of the 160-acre irrigation limitation for water provided by Bureau of Reclamation projects as stipulated in the Reclamation Act of 1902 and subsequent legislation. This would have the salutary effect of bringing agriculture in large areas of the West into smaller, more energy-efficient units and increasing both production and the rural economy in the affected areas.

10. *Financing Small Farms.* There should be an immediate assessment of the feasibility of utilizing financial machinery used to revive agriculture in the 1930s (e.g., the Farm Security Administration, Federal Land Banks, Federal Intermediate Credit Act, Production Credit Administration) to get financial and technical aid to small family farmers.

11. *Decentralize the U.S. Department of Agriculture.* The USDA, to be maximally effective, should be regionalized, as have other departments and agencies, and with its regional offices decentralized further into state offices charged with bringing about maximum conservation of energy, water, and soil resources. Farmer-elected committees should assist the offices in setting priorities in keeping with local, state, and national objectives.

12. *Urban Food Production.* Urban, suburban, and small-town food production units with local controls, and community processing kitchens in churches and other community facilities are needed badly. They could easily utilize publicly-owned, leased land, and land in utility and transportation rights-of-way.

13. *Land Banking.* There should be established a system of land banking, with semi-autonomous local controls, to permit the purchase of agricultural and timber lands coming on the market, encourage water and land conservation, and allow the leasing of the land for production of needed crops by family-sized or cooperative units on long-term, inheritable rental contracts similar to those used in Israel.

14. *Decentralize Feedlots.* The establishment or maintenance of feedlots of a size or location which precludes the full utilization of manures and other wastes on agricultural land within easy hauling distance should be prohibited. This would have the effect also of some decentralization of abattoirs, thus reducing long, energy-expensive hauls of meats.

15. *Fertilizer/Water Priorities*. Fertilizer and water use must be prohibited for such nonessentials as lawns on both public and private property, cemeteries, golf courses, highway median strips, and rights-of-way. Grass and plants which require such treatment should be replaced with those which do not, but which perform the essential functions of preventing erosion.

16. *Geothermal Energy*. Geothermal resources should be established by legislation as national resources, to be administered locally by interconnecting, community-controlled corporations. (It should be pointed out here that geothermal energy has barely begun to be tapped and that heat-pump methods of utilizing earth temperature differences of a very few degrees have been successfully tested, making its use theoretically possible in virtually every state of the nation.)

17. *Aquaculture*. A national policy of priorities on fish and mollusk farming should be established and funded for development of freshwater and marine aquaculture. Revolutionary techniques in production of salt water mussels, in particular, are being developed in Puget Sound, in estuarial bays of Spain, and in Japan, and indicate that vast quantities (as much as 500,000 pounds per acre annually) of high protein mussel meat can be produced. This can be done without disturbing the ecology of the seawater. The mussel meat can be converted into food for human consumption, protein concentrates for livestock, and food for fish being grown in marine and freshwater enclosures. Computations of potential production, based on output of test installations, indicate the gap between production and protein needs of the population of 1990 could be closed entirely by mussel production and oyster production utilizing similar techniques. Also, increases in development capital could shorten that interval considerably.

References

Adelman, I. and C.T. Morris. "Anatomy of Income Distribution Patterns in Developing Countries." *Development Digest*, October 1971.

Agribusiness Accountability Project. *Hard Times, Hard Tomatoes: The Failure of the Land Grant College Complex*. Paperback book. Available from the Agribusiness Accountability Project, 1000 Wisconsin Ave., N.W., Washington, D.C.

Anderson, William D.; Gustafson, Gregory C.; and Boxley, F. "Perspectives on Agricultural Policy." Paper to be published in November-December Special Issue of *The Journal of Soil and Water Conservation*, 1974.

Baker, John. *What Is Rural Development?* Bemidji, Minnesota: Northern Minnesota Coordinating Council, 1972.

Beale, Calvin. *Rural and Non-Metropolitan Trends of Significance to National Population Policy*. Testimony before the U.S. Senate Subcommittee on Rural Development. U.S. Senate. October 28, 1973.

Benne, E.J. et al. Michigan Agricultural Experiment Station Circular Bull., No. 231, 1961.

Berg, Alan D. *The Nutrition Factor*. The Brooking Institution. A study sponsored by the Foundation for Child Development.

Black Economic Research Center. *Only Six Million Acres: The Decline of Black Owned Land in the Rural South*. New York: The Black Economic Research Center, 1973.

Borlaug, Norman. Testimony before the Select Committee on Nutrition and Human Needs in the U.S. Senate. Washington, D.C., June 14, 1974.

Bowden, B.D. Lee. "The Neglected Human Factor." *American Journal of Agricultural Economics*, 55 (December 1973): 879-887.

Boxley, Robert F. and Anderson, William D., "The Incidence of Benefits from Commodity Price-Support Programs: A Case Study of Tobacco." In *Government Spending and Land Values: Public Money and Private Gain*, ed. by C. Lowell Harris. Madison: The University of Wisconsin Press, 1973.

Brown, Lester R. Article in the *Wall Street Journal*, October 10, 1973.

Brown, Lester R. "The Next Crisis? Food." *Foreign Policy*, No. 13 (Winter 1973-74): 3-33.

Brown, Lester R. "Global Food Insecurity." *The Futurist* (April 1974): 56-64.

Bryson, Reid. "Climatic Change and Drought in the Monsoon Lands." Paper given at the AAAS meeting, University of Wisconsin, in February 1974.

Bureau of Census, United States. *World Population: 1973*. ISP/WP-73. Washington, D.C., 1974. 11 pp.

Butz, Earl L. "We Need a Higher Level of Economic Literacy." Address before the Mid-Winter Convention of the Oklahoma Press Association, Oklahoma City, Oklahoma, February 15, 1974.

Campbell, Phil. *Cooperatives: A Necessity for Family Farms*. From *Ag. Alert*. November 14, 1974, p. 19.

Chapman, H.O. and J.G. Youde. *Some Impacts of the Changing Energy Situation on U.S. Agriculture*. Paper given at the 1974 AAEX meetings in College Station, Texas.

Clark, Dick. *Progress and Plans for Implementation of Rural Development*. 93rd Congress, 1st Session. Washington, D.C.: Committee Print, 1975.

Cochrane, Willard W. *Feast or Famine: The Uncertain World of Food & Agriculture and Its Policy Implications to the U.S.* Washington, D.C.: National Planning Association, 1974.

Commission on Population Growth and the American Future. *Population Growth and the American Future*. Interim Report. Washington, D.C.: U.S. Govt. Printing Office, 1971.

Dept. of Health, Education, and Welfare. Health Services and Mental Health Administration. Center for Disease Control. *Ten-State Nutrition Survey, 1968-70*. Atlanta, Georgia, 1972.

Dupree, W.G., Jr., and J.A. West. *United States Energy Through the Year 2000*. U.S. Dept. of Interior, December 1972.

Economic Tables. USDA ERS-559 Economic Research Service.

Farm Population Estimates 1910-1970. USDA Rural Development Service. Statistical Bulletin No. 523. July 1973.

Food and Agricultural Organization. *Energy & Protein Requirements.* Report of a Joint FAO/WHO ad hoc export committee. Rome, 1973.

Food and Agricultural Organization. *Preliminary Assessment of the World Food Situation Present and Future.* E/CONF 65/Prep 6, Rome, April 1974.

Food and Agricultural Organization. *The World Food Problem, Proposals for National and International Action.* E/CONF 65/4, F.A.O., Rome, August 1974.

Food & Nutrition Board Report. *Recommended Dietary Allowances.* 8th Edition. Washington, D.C.: National Research Council, National Academy of Sciences, 1973.

Goldberg, D. and Shmueh, M. *Drip Irrigation—A Method Used Under Arid and Desert Conditions of High Water and Soil Salinity.* Transcript from the American Society of Agricultural Engineers. Vol. 13, 1970, pp. 38-41.

Goldschmidt, Walter. Statement before the Subcommittee on Monopoly of the U.S. Senate, 92nd Congress, Second Session, Washington, D.C.: U.S. Government Printing Office, March 1, 1972.

Grant, James P. *Growth from Below: A People Oriented Development Strategy.* Overseas Development Council, Development Paper #16. December 1973, 29 pp.

Hall, D.W. *Handling and Storage of Food Grains in Tropical and Subtropical Areas.* F.A.O. Rome, 1970.

Heady, Earl et al. *American Farm Size and Structure.* The Center for Agriculture and Rural Development.Iowa State University, Report #48. 1974.

Heichel, G.H. *Comparative Efficiency of Energy Use in Crop Production.* The Connecticut Agricultural Experiment Station. Bulletin 739. New Haven, Connecticut, November 1973.

Hirst, Eric. *Energy Use for Food in the United States.* Oak Ridge National Laboratory. Oak Ridge, Tennessee, 1973.

Household Food Consumption, 1955. Report #16 USDA *Dietary Evaluation of Food Used in Households in the United States.* Washington, D.C., U.S. Government Printing Office, November 1961.

Household Food Consumption Survey, 1965-66. Report #6 USDA *Dietary Levels of Households in the United States.* Washington, D.C., July 1969.

JT. Study. California Dept. of Food and Agriculture and the University of California. *Energy Requirements for Agriculture in California.* Davis, California, January 1974.

Krause, K.R., and Kyle, L.R., *Midwestern Corn Farms: Economic Status and the Potential for Large and Family Sized Units.* Agricultural Economy Report No. 216, ERS-USDA, 1973.

Lappe, Francis Moore. "The World Food Problem." *Commonwealth* 99 (February 8, 1974): 457-59.

La Rose, Bruce L. "Arvin & Dinuba Revisited." University of Minnesota, Department of Agricultural Economics, March 1970. Manuscript.

Larson, Donald K. "Economic Class of Farm and the Farm Family Welfare Myth." Contributed paper to American Agriculture Economics Association Meetings, College Station, Texas, August 1974.

Madden, J. Patrick. *Economics of Size in Farming.* Agricultural Economy Report No. 107, ERS-USDA, 1967.

May, Jacques M., and Hoty Lemons. "The Ecology of Malnutrition." *Jour. Am. Med. Assn.* 207, 13 (March 13, 1969): 2401-2404.

Miller, Judith. "Agriculture: FDA Seeks to Regulate Genetic Manipulation of Food Crops." *Science* 185 (July 19, 1974): 240-242.

Morrison, F.P. *Feeds & Feeding.* Ithaca, N.Y.: Henry & Morrison, 1946, pp. 50 and 429.

Nikolitch, Radoje. *Family-Size Farms in U.S. Agriculture.* ERS-499, ERS-USDA, 1972.

Paulson, Arnold E. "Lessons of History—Past, Present, and Future About the Earth's Resources." In *Central Issues in Agricultural Policy.* Columbia: Report of Seminar Sponsored by M.G. and Johnnye D. Perry Foundation and University of Missouri. Special Report 163, 1974.

Perelman, Michael. "Efficiency in Agriculture." Testimony before Subcommittee on Migratory Labor. San Francisco, California, January 11, 1972.

Pimentel, David et al. "Food Production and the Energy Crisis." *Science* 182, 4111 (November 2, 1973): 443-449.

Population Reference Bureau, Inc. *1973 World Population Data Sheet.* 1755 Massachusetts Avenue NW, Washington, D.C.

President's Science Advisory Committee. *The World Food Problem.* Report of the Panel on the World Food Supply. Vol. 1. Washington, D.C.: U.S. Govt. Printing Office, 1967.

President's Science Advisory Committee. Panel on the World Food Supply. *The World Food Problem.* Vol. 2. Washington, D.C.: U.S. Govt. Printing Office, 1967.

Raup, Phillip. "Some Issues Raised by Structural Changes in American Agriculture." Testimony prepared for hearings before the Subcommittee on Migratory Labor. Washington, D.C.: U.S. Government Printing Office, November 5, 1971, pp. 605-635.

Raup, Phillip. "Needed Research into the Effects of Large Scale Farm and Business Firms on Rural America." Testimony before the U.S. Senate Subcommittee on Monopoly. Washington, D.C.: U.S. Govt. Printing Office, March 1, 1972.

Rosenfeld, Stephen S. "The Politics of Food." *Foreign Policy* 14 (Spring 1974): 17-29.

Salamon, Lester M. *Black-Owned Land: Profile of a Disappearing Equity Base.* Report to the Office of Minority Business Enterprise, U.S. Department of Commerce, 1974.

Schertz, Lyle. "World Food: Prices and the Poor." *Foreign Affairs* (April 1974): 511-537.

Schneeberger, K.C. and West, J.G. "Marginal Farms—A Micro Development Opportunity." *Southern Journal of Agricultural Economics* 4, 1 (July 1972): 97-100.

Schneeberger, K.C.; West, J.G.; Osburn, D.C.; and Hartman, J. "Expanding Agricultural Production: The Small Farmer Case," Contribution from the Missouri Agricultural Experiment Station. Journal Series #7022.

Schneeberger, K.C. et al. "Expanding Agricultural Production: The Small Farmer Case." Missouri Agricultural Experiment Station. Journal Series #7022. Columbia, Mo.

Schumacher, E.F. *Small Is Beautiful—Economics As If People Mattered.* San Francisco: Harper Torchbooks, 1973.

Senate, U.S. Hearing Before the Senate Select Committee on Nutrition and Human Needs. Pt. 1. *Famine & The World Situation.* Sen. George McGovern, Chairman.

Senate, U.S. Select Committee on Nutrition & Human Needs. Panel Report: *Nutrition and the International Situation.* Washington, D.C.: U.S. Govt. Printing Office, June 1974.

Stansel, J.W. *Climatic Impact Assessment Program—Rice.* Monograph V, Chapter 4, Section 4.3.1.c. Texas A&M University. November 1973.

Steinhart, John S. and Carole. "Energy Use in the U.S. Food System." *Science* 184 (April 19, 1974): 307-316.

Stevenson, Adlai III. Statement before the U.S. Senate Subcommittee on Migratory Labor. Washington, D.C.: U.S. Govt. Printing Office, November 5, 1971.

Sunquest, W.D. et al. *Who Controls Agriculture Now?* The Trends Underway. North Central Regional Extension Publication #32. University of Illinois, 1972.

Talmadge, Herman E., *Explanation of the Rural Development Act of 1972*, Public Law 92-419, Committee on Agriculture and Forestry, United States Senate, 93rd Congress, 2nd Session. Washington, D.C.: U.S. Govt. Printing Office, 1972.

Tisdale, S.L. and W.L. Nelson. *Soil Fertility and Fertilizers.* New York: Macmillan, 1966.

Tolley, George S. "Management Entry into U.S. Agriculture." *American Journal of Agricultural Economics* 52 (November 1970): 485-493.

U.S. Bureau of the Census, *Census of Agriculture*, 1969.

U.S. Congress. Senate Select Comm. on Nutrition and Human Needs. *National Nutrition Policy Study. Report & Recommendations—IV.* Washington, D.C.: U.S. Govt. Printing Office, June 1974.

U.S. Dept. of Agriculture. *Economics of Size in Farming.* Agricultural Report #107, Economic Research Service. Washington, D.C.

U.S. Dept. of Agriculture. *Changes in Farm Production & Efficiency: A*

Summary Report. Economic Research Survey Statistical Bulletin #233, June 1972.

U.S. Dept. of Agriculture. "The One-Man Farm." ERS-519. Economic Research Service. Washington, D.C., August 1973.

U.S. Dept. of Agriculture. Economic Research Service. *The World Food Situation.* October 1974.

U.S. Dept. of Commerce. *Farm Population Census Series.* ERS. #45. September 1974, p. 27.

U.S. Senate. Select Committee on Nutrition & Human Needs. *Report on Nutrition & The International Situation.* Washington, D.C.: Govt. Printing Office, September 1974.

United Nations, Food and Agricultural Organization. *Provisional Indicative World Plan for Agricultural Development.* (I.W.P.) Vol. 1. Rome, 1970.

United Nations, Food and Agricultural Organization. *Perspective Plan for Agricultural Development and Integration in Central America.* Unreleased Report. 1973.

United Nations, Food and Agricultural Organization. *The State of Food & Agriculture,* 1973. pp. 21-34.

United Nations, Population Division, Dept. of Economics and Social Affairs. *World Population Prospects, 1965-2000 as Assessed in 1968.* ESA/P/WP. 37, 17 (December 1970).

University of California Food Task Force. *A Hungry World: The Challenge of Agriculture.* Div. of Agricultural Sciences, University of California, July 1974.

Walker, Martin. "Drought." *New York Times Magazine* (June 9, 1974).

Wardle, Christopher, and Boisvert, Richard N. "Farm and Non-Farm Alternatives for Limited Resource Dairy Farmers in Central New York," A.E. Research 74-6, Cornell University, Ithaca, New York, 1974.

West, Quentin M. "The World Food Situation—And How Others See It." Speech at a Conference on International Agricultural Training. Airlie, Virginia, April 3, 1974.

Willett, Joseph W. "The Ability of the Developing Countries to Meet Their Own Agricultural Needs in the 1980's." Speech given at the Canadian Agricultural Economics Society Meeting. Published by USDA Quebec City, Canada, August 6, 1974.

Wittwer, S.H. *Some Environmental Ecological ... Aspects of Crop Production in Greenhouses.* Proc. CIGR Meeting Agricultural Engineering and Environment. Aachen, Germany, September 6-7, 1973.

Wittwer, S.H. "Maximum Production Capacity of Food Crops." *Bio-Science* 24, 4 (April 1974): 216-224.

V

Agriculture: Where We Are Going

Stewart Bledsoe

One of today's phenomena is an increasing awareness of the limitations on world food supplies, but when the question is asked, "Where is America going in agriculture?" the answer is unbelievable—"Nowhere." After an exhaustive sampling of the agricultural community, I am unable to find *any* agri-business-man who feels that there have been *any* national goals established *by agriculturists, for agriculture.* This incomprehensible vacuum is suicidal. And it points out the absolute necessity of rectifying this amoebic posture soon.

As a nation, we have shown an unprecedented ability to accomplish amazing things when we take the trouble to lay out firm goals and anchor them to definite timetables. When President Kennedy established the Space Program and set a firm date when our country would have a man on the moon, there were severe limitations on our technical capability to accomplish the goal. But we hit the target date exactly as the result of a national determination and rearrangement of priorities to accomplish an understood goal. Our entry into the nuclear field—first in weaponry, and then the application of the nuclear capability to peaceful uses—also involved an all-out drive to accomplish agreed upon goals by certain deadlines. Americans are driving coast to coast on an interstate system which did not exist until we assumed the responsibility as a nation for establishing a freeway system. These examples, and others, point out the ability to turn the same page in history as far as agriculture is concerned, if we give the issue the emphasis that current events dictate and the priority that it deserves.

As of today, the national goals for agribusiness are unstated, undefined, and without timetables. Their definition is of critical importance. Based on the

113

alternatives available and the level of productivity decided upon, the national goal for agriculture could fall into one of three suggested categories.

Alternative A: "Stand Pat"

We could decide to continue our present pace. This is certainly the line of least resistance and the one which would require the least *short-range* discomfort and awkwardness. But even when balanced against the natural increases in productivity which gradually accumulating technology and know-how would effect, a continuation of our present posture will yield little increase. The disappearance of an estimated one million acres per year to highways, airports, and housing developments is even now beginning to show an effect on the productivity side of the ledger. Prime farmlands, which are disappearing under asphalt at an alarming rate, are gone forever.

Soil erosion as a spinoff of improper farming, and fertility-robbing practices such as improper irrigation, drainage, and other misapplications have cost us millions of acres in the past. Amazingly enough, in this age of technical know-how, these practices still continue and, without a major determination that they will be corrected, can be expected to be with us into the future. The concomitant loss of the end product—dependable and economic farm production—will come back to haunt us one day.

Much of the increase in agricultural productivity we have enjoyed in the last decade has been dependent on a steady supply of production inputs—human capability, adequate credit, petrochemicals, and energy. Unless such supplies are protected in the future by a national goal, however, other interests backed by urban political clout will overwhelm agriculture in competition for these increasingly scarce items.

It must be accepted that the energy crunch is a long-range problem, and that conservation measures are essential. Given this situation, agriculture will undoubtedly suffer unless a firm determination is made early on that it is to receive sufficient energy allocations, for no other agricultural input is more productivity-related than the petrochemical spectrum. The green revolution was built on petrochemicals. Without national commitment to agricultural diversion of the natural gas fraction (2 percent) needed for the production of anhydrous ammonia, the yield per acre of many of our crops would drop to pre-World War Two levels. The shock of this production-recession would shake our economy almost as violently as the petroleum recession.

There must be a concomitant commitment to the use of pesticides, herbicides, and other chemical inputs if even present levels of production are to be maintained. The present practice of continually withdrawing productivity-oriented chemicals by government fiat needs a reappraisal. America's understandable dream of an unsullied environment carries with it a substantial economic impact in its accomplishment. Any discussion of environmental impacts must carry with it an equally searching investigation of the economic impacts of environmental purity. Such has not been the case before. It must be a part of any future environmental considerations.

An adequate supply of capital is one of the major factors which has propelled our agricultural productivity into stratospheric heights, particularly when viewed from the production levels of our political competitor, the Soviet Union. We have had a steady supply of risk capital to finance our technological break-throughs. Today's money crunch finds the credit flooring for continued agricultural expansion seriously curtailed. If we are to maintain any serious production advances in the future, some reassessment of our credit priorities is in order. If such is not done, even though the technology is on the shelf, chemicals in the tank, and land available for production commitments, nothing is going to ensue without front money. Of equal importance is the reappraisal of the credit system which may provide adequate inputs for long-range finance but leaves agriculture woefully short of mid-term capital. Without some improvement of the mid-term capability, the daily operations will of necessity be hand-to-mouth operations instead of something properly planned.

Also threatened by higher-levered competitive opportunities is the human replacement for today's rapidly aging farmer. He now averages fifty-two years. Unless there can be a greater expectation that agriculture will return as good a living as the same talents would provide "in town," today's agriculture work force will be even more superannuated in another decade. Let's not be blinded by the current wave of young back-to-the-soil organicists or urban pea-patch gardeners. The agriculturists who will expand America's production potential must be the same hard-driving, well-educated, money-smart young innovators who are actively bid for by industry, professions, and government. Agriculture cannot expand without this now desperately needed human transfusion.

Summary of Alternative A: "Stand Pat"

Alternative A is a relatively painless and easy out, but while it has some surface feel of progress, it is a booby trap. Back-door losses will more than offset productivity advances if these are acquired at the present rate. Settling for a "Stand Pat" position, or even worse—drifting along with no determination—will come back to haunt us one day. By that time, it could be too late, for we will have an overaged farm force and insufficient qualified replacements in sight.

**Alternative B: The Expansion Necessary for a
Continued "Good-Life America"**

With only a minor shakeup of existing priority arrangements, by merely following up on previous lip service, we could regain some national momentum that will be necessary if our country is to enjoy "agribusiness as usual" for the next two decades. Some of the most obvious areas for attention come to mind when the shift of emphasis away from agriculture is reexamined.

Bringing desert lands in the West under irrigation has been a winner. It has also fallen into disfavor during the mid-1950 periods of agricultural surpluses and the shift in priorities away from land reclamation to inner city human reclamation. As a result of this deemphasis, federal funds that were appropriated in a most niggardly fashion for a small handful of irrigation startups were subsequently frozen by an administration which had other more important fish to fry. If these funds were reappropriated and released by the administration for irrigation construction starts, we could increase our inventory of productive lands to an amazing degree. Upgrading production per acre by 300 to 1000 percent has to have an impact when we are looking at a potential acreage in the millions.

The annual farm land disappearance has been a little noted tragedy. The manner in which some of it has been misused constitutes a national disgrace. Immediate enactment by Congress of land-use planning legislation, which has the maximum involvement of local governmental agencies and open avenues of citizen participation, can check this tide. Let no one delude himself into thinking that all land diversion will automatically be stopped. Nor should it be. But the mindless ripoff which has marked the development pattern of the mid-twentieth century will prove to be disastrously expensive for subsequent generations. No magic wand, waved from Washington, D.C., will automatically correct this. But manpower and womanpower to do it is available at the local level, given the tools and the guidelines, and a well-timed jab with a sharp stick.

The present dollar commitments to agricultural research in less newsworthy areas such as genetics, soil chemistry, agricultural cybernetics, soils management, etc., have been difficult to maintain. In some instances, the percentage set aside for desperately needed production answers has diminished. It is estimated that even a modest elevation of research emphasis in agriculture-related fields would increase productivity on *present* acreage by 10 to 15 percent. It is unrealistic to count on productivity increases exceeding that amount unless there is a major reallocation of research priorities and a reemphasis, backed with cash, of the idea that "research pays off." A *major* effort is needed in research agriculture which at least equals inquiry into social, medical, technical, and electronic research areas.

With the prospect of an extended energy shortage, it is mandatory that there be an ironclad guarantee of not only supply but delivery of energy and petrochemicals essential for the agricultural expansion necessary to maintain a "Good-Life America." It must be understood that today's agricultural energy commitment consists of little more than a place near the head of the line forming before the energy pay-window. When the agriculturist arrives at the wicket and the energy master says, "Sorry, we are all out today" and closes the window, all the assurances of supply are pretty hollow. It is delivery that counts. And this can only be guaranteed by an affirmation of the guarantees of supply *and* delivery from the highest level. Petrochemicals are very much a part of this. Without the petrochemical commitment, the miserable spectre of more gallons of fuel being consumed per bushel of grain raised becomes a definite possibility, as yields per acre drop off—a pitiful commentary on our energy/petrochemical sophistication in an era which bills itself as enlightened.

There must also be a continuing emphasis on foreign market development. For a nation which once had the worldwide pseudonym of "Yankee Traders," our foreign market development effort is pretty pitiful now. There are some success stories, but these are matched by many other spastic performances from both the governmental and the private sectors.

The machinery exists on paper, but federal efforts too often only shuffle these papers, instead of bird-dogging trade prospects. It is also mandatory that we send in the "A-Team." A case in point: Agricultural attache in the Soviet Union (a USDA type) whom I met was a victim of a bureaucratic career. His vision of what was happening in agriculture in the Soviet Union was dim. His understanding of what was really happening in American agriculture wasn't much brighter. He would never have made the grade with the private sector unless he possessed qualities I did not perceive in an admittedly short meeting. But when you go up against the Russian trade officials, there is no question that you are dealing with their best minds. It seems only reasonable that if we are serious about foreign trade expansion, we should trot out our best trade-expanders.

Even for a nation which is one of the food brokers for the world, we still do not produce everything we consume. We must import food in order to maintain our food options at their present level. Our nation grows no cocoa, coffee, and only part of its sugar. And what better payment for an agricultural import than an agricultural export. And what better payment for high-priced energy from the Middle East than American foodstuffs. Let's face it. We have tried paying for those with dollars and *that* doesn't work. Until we aggressively exercise foreign market development, it is still going to be hard work to pay for the energy and/or food imports which we must have to live.

Our transportation arteries are superannuated and sclerotic. The perishability of market agricultural commodities requires modern transportation. To even out the peaks and valleys of domestic distribution, a massive revitalizing of a worn-out rail transportation system will be required, and soon. Paralleling the revitalization of the existing system, there must be a commitment to explore new transportation possibilities—e.g., containerization of cargoes, palletizing and concentration of bulk agricultural commodities in the field, and air freight as a daily tool rather than a once-a-season publicity stunt. There is nothing about this effort that will come cheap. But, like putting off a visit to the dentist, continued delay will result in a transportation system that is even worse than it is today.

Over the last decade, some regressive legislative and administrative policies emerging from Congress have stifled agricultural expansion. Among these are some of the GATT arrangements, which have exploited American agriculture. In our desire to be a "good fellow," we have allowed other nations to use agriculture as a football to kick up and down the field during the warm-up period. The day must stop when American agriculture is used as a diplomatic "Loss-Leader."

The current pygmy status of our maritime fleet is a direct outgrowth of the Jones Act—a protective anachronism from a different era. This measure, conceived in conspiracy and born out of an unholy shipowner-labor leader-ship-builder alliance, has reduced our ability to move American commodities in American ships to levels which would be laughable if they were not so tragic. There is nothing wrong with our transportation industry that the repeal of some protective legislation would not improve. The same holds true, incidentally, for import restrictions and many of our tariffs, quotas, and other restrictive impedimenta.

Summary of Alternative B: The Expansion Necessary
for a Continued "Good-Life America"

This alternative would be costly and set some teeth on edge. Most of the pieces necessary to construct the agricultural expansion necessary for continued "Good-Life America" are already in hand, unimplemented, or are on the drawing board. In a crisis-oriented system, it will probably take a crisis to produce the determination to cover the waterfront on these proposals—and that moment is fast approaching. But it is still do-able even without a crisis, given sufficient drive on the part of agribusiness leadership and government catalyzers.

Alternative C: Go For Broke—Why
Should We? How Should We?

This alternative is scary and risk-fraught, but the potential rewards make it worth a good, long look. First, it is an integral part of Operation Independence. The target date for arrival at this energy Nirvana is in the mid-1980s. And how are we to finance our high-priced imports from the OPEC cartels in the interim? The first one that comes to mind is by export of our largest negotiable export commodity—agricultural products. The world is undersupplied with food. Many areas of the world now have hard currency to buy food-stuffs some place. Why not from us? A case in point: The Middle East imports 90 percent of its food. Why should we not be their supplier? It seems reasonable that we pay for high-priced oil with high-priced wheat? That is not too bad a trade.

The spectre of worldwide hunger grows daily more visible. And Malthus is becoming an established and proven prophet—he predicted the overpopulation, which is obviously not going to disappear overnight. With population expected to increase by 2 percent per year until the year 2000, it is estimated that the developing nations will need two to three times their present 25,000,000 tons of annual food imports. Unless some serious thinking goes into a resolution of this problem, it will loom on the horizon one day soon as a major international crisis. If the present trend continues unattended, arable land areas in the world will decrease. With the rise in energy costs and continued maldistribution of population related to sources of food, the world is faced with two unsatisfactory alternatives: (1) The prospect of frequent mass deaths, or (2) continued diversion of more and more of the world's income to food, leaving less available for anything else to maintain civilization as we now know it.

Some serious homework must go into developing a negotiable system of international grain reserves *and* concessional finance which can guarantee up to ten million tons per year for developing nations. Along with this must come international commitments from the developing nations, and also the "have" nations, which will increase the productivity of those who "have not." While the potential for many of the developing nations to achieve self-sufficiency is sharply limited by climactic constraints and/or population maldistribution, there still must be a definable effort made by them and for them to achieve a greater degree of self-sufficiency. Without evidence of such a commitment, the contributing nations will soon grow tired of their role and we are right back in the soup again.

No one can ignore the fact that the "have not" hungry nations are rapidly acquiring capability to put a nuclear gun to the "have" nations' heads. The ability to deliver nuclear weapons by conventional or MIRV systems becomes less important daily. An atom bomb can be fitted into a trunk and shipped to Washington, D.C., with its arrival to coincide with a "Deliver Food" ultimatum. The "have not" nations now have the capability to sit down across the bargaining table from the "haves" and state factually, "We want what you've got and we have the muscle to take it." From there, it's not too broad a jump from a Boeing 747 highjacking to an international food heist and finally to a food-motivated anarchy. If we are to respond with supplies before these not-too-farfetched horrors become realities, then we must increase our national commitment to become a dependable large-scale world food source.

No citizen from a nation priding itself on a Christian ethic can take comfort from the present horror of 10,000 people a week dying of hunger somewhere in this world—particularly when the United States could participate meaningfully in saving more of them. It is a pitiful irrationality that we waste more in this country than many nations have, and that what we throw away, properly conserved, would be sufficient to save those 10,000 who die every week.

No one can ignore the problems of *who* pays and *how* they pay, and of devising a workable delivery mechanism. Unfortunately, however, these issues are the subject of too much rhetoric now. The bombastic performance at the recent World Food Conference in Rome was a depressing tragicomedy. The political one-upmanship being practiced there by people who should have known better must have seemed insane to those who were about to starve. The best minds, both national and international, must be committed to devising some scheme in which all the "have" nations will contribute something to a world depository. If that is food, fine. If it cannot be food, then let it be oil, or minerals, or *something*. We can hope that this kind of planning can be done without the infantile political bickerings which have marked such discussions in the past. At this point, it is wise to bind ourselves nationally to the maxim that "Any goal can be accomplished as long as you do not care who gets credit."

The game plan for solving the aforementioned problems must accompany, if not precede, any national productivity-increasing commitment which is dedicated largely to saving the starving. If we produce these surpluses for distribution without equal commitments of contributions in kind from our nonagricultural but oil or mineral-wealthy neighbors, we will find our agricultural accumulation weakening any leverage we might have to spur their participation.

It is also at the outset, rather than at the conclusion, of this program that the "have" nations can and must insist that any nation seeking a withdrawal from the world food bank must have in hand a firmed-up action plan of what they plan to do for themselves about their runaway population expansion. The fascination with procreation in the "have not" nations places an intolerable burden on those who would commit themselves to feeding them. With two-thirds of the population growth in the last decade occurring in the one-third of the nations at the lowest end of the food production spectrum, it is obvious that our priorities are askew. But to make population control workable, we must place the order before we get to the bottom line on any delivery commitment. It sounds cruel, but without such a commitment, we are saving today's millions only to condemn their descendants to death.

One of the more compelling reasons for going-for-broke as a national priority is that agricultural exports may be continued indefinitely with proper management. Given the application of modern technology, modern farming practices, and a real emphasis on some of the old discarded simplistics like manure conservation, plowing under crop residues, and carefully planned soil-enriching crop rotations, we could wind up richer in our natural resources after a decade of heavy emphasis on full production. The sad commentary on metals, most chemicals, and our petroleum reserves is this: When they are gone, they are *gone*. Fortunately, this need not be the case with agricultural production.

Summary of Alternative C: Go For Broke

Alternative C will be very expensive and very controversial. The population control issue, the nuts-and-bolts problems of who pays for the food diverted to the have-not nations and the thorny issues of who handles the food bank are explosive concepts. They are fraught with pitfalls and suspicion and will be resisted by many people. Perhaps it is too much for our nation to "go for broke" in one jump, but we are overdue for some tentative "first steps."

Conclusions

Any future game plan will have to choose among these three alternatives. As stated before, the position we should assume on this spectrum has never been seriously considered as a defined national priority. The future food balance of this planet, and the role of our nation in it, is of sufficient immediacy that it deserves serious thought by the best minds available. One stage of this agricultural reappraisal should be a full and extended debate by the Congress so that a national policy can be formulated. Goals must be established and cutoff dates agreed to for accomplishing segments of the game plan. The price that we will all pay for continued drift could be horrendous. Amazingly enough, in the agricultural area, one of the critical choices that Americans have to make is whether to choose a course at all. We have not even taken a first step so far.

In all these discussions, the temptation must be resisted to view agriculture as a public utility. It must be continually stressed that agriculture is anything *but* that. Any governmentalist who falls into that mode of appraisal dooms his planning and himself to failure. The profitability, the market system, the efficiency-producing incentives must remain in agriculture and must be reinforced at every turn, for, in the last analysis, these are the magic ingredients of America's green revolution. Even granting the natural benefits that are ours, the rich soil and favorable climate, the true yeast that makes the agricultural dough rise is the ingenuity, productivity, and motivation of a unique American businessman—the American farmer. He will not be molded. Many have tried to buy him, without success; and those who have tried to regiment him have wound up sadder but wiser. So the national goals established, at least in part, at the governmental level must never lose sight of the fact that government itself cannot farm. That has been proven decisively by the largest government-farmer in the world—the USSR. But the American *farmer* can farm—as well or better than anyone in the world. Given the proper opportunities and the expression of a national determination, his response could confound even the most optimistic planners.

Present domestic rural rehabilitation programs, which have attempted to reverse the migration from rural America to urban America, have continually dealt with symptoms rather than the single root cause. The favorable farm gate prices of the last few years have of themselves done more to reverse this trend than all the relocation, retraining, and redirecting accomplished in the previous decade. People did not leave rural America because they wished to. They had no choice. Given an opportunity to stay, they reversed the trend dramatically. In the same period, enrollments in colleges of agriculture have increased as well. On some land grant campuses, those enrollments have risen by 250 percent, something that no previous recruiting programs or blandishments could contrive.

Also worth attention in long-range planning is finding some alternative to the boom-or-bust cycle which plagues many agricultural commodities today. The farmer who is compelled to say every year, with dice in hand, "I'll roll you for the ranch, the kids' future, and everything I got, double or nothing," is a real anachronism. No one else in today's economy does anything close to it. Small wonder that agriculture is having a difficult time attracting and retaining replacements. One of the basic problems, however, is that once into a managed supply-economy, particularly if government is doing the management, incentive diminishes and productivity drops. The answer might be found in farmer-operated marketing schemes, farmer bargaining associations, and other devices which can balance the producer's clout as the farmer enters pricing negotiations with overpoweringly strong processors.

Discussions leading to definitions of a national agricultural policy must not take on the aspect of another set of calisthenics, however. Neither agriculture, the American public, nor its Congress are much interested in these anymore. If we are talking about devising a game plan to which we will commit ourselves as a nation, with priority rearrangements and agreed target dates, that is another thing. We are all the beneficiaries of the priority restructuring (educational, metallurgical, technological, and developmental) that produced the lunar project. Agricultural production goal-setting can have immediate and long-range benefits that could exceed anything affirmative that we have seen from the original Manhattan Project, reclamation projects, or any of the other natural resource multiplying ventures that our nation has considered since its infancy.

It is my proposal that any serious attention to this goal-setting and highlighting of the nuts and bolts needed to accomplish these goals, concentrate on the alternatives before us in Alternative B, some expansion, or Alternative C, a full commitment. Anything less than these is Band-Aid economics anyway.

VI

Energy and Environment as Allies: Suggestions for Unified Action on Both Crises

Henry L. Diamond

From the late 60s through 1973, environmentalists in the United States won an almost unbroken string of victories. After many years of crying in the wilderness, major new legislation was enacted to clean up the water and the air and to care for the land better. Moreover, environmental quality was set forth as a national goal of high priority in the National Environmental Policy Act of 1970. That act created machinery such as the environmental impact statement to ensure that the nation made progress toward the goal which Congress established.

This era of good feeling was abruptly shaken by the OPEC oil embargo of 1973. Some of the first substitutes for Arab oil were aggressive attacks on the environment. It was proposed to cut air quality standards to allow for high sulphur oil; it was proposed to step up strip mining and offshore oil drilling without environmental safeguards; and it was proposed to speed up nuclear power production dramatically.

For their part, the environmentalists tended to dig in their heels to protect new and hard-won victories. They strongly, and for the most part successfully, resisted changes in the Clean Air Act, and continued to push a tough federal strip-mining bill despite waving of the energy crisis flag by the opposition.

The controversy still simmers in oil company advertisements and in press releases of the ecologists. But, as the slightly sulphur-laden smoke begins to clear, it appears that energy and environmental needs may be more compatible

This chapter appeared in the *New York Times*, October 29, 1974 and has been brought up to date. ©1974 by the New York Times Company. Reprinted by permission.

than anyone suspected. In fact, it may be that the two potential adversaries might turn out to be allies.

The environmental movement may be able to offer the basic approach to the energy problem which provides the fastest and cheapest energy savings—old-fashioned conservation. Before it entered an era of fashionability, the ecological movement was called conservation. It advocated wise use of resources and wasting not.

In postwar affluence, this traditional theme got lost. Amid the rush to a trillion-dollar gross national product, personal and national thrift went the way of the rumble seat. The conservationists changed and became environmentalists concerned with water and air pollution and the effluents of affluence.

The oil embargo of 1973-74 might help revive this American tradition of saving, for conservation offers the fastest and surest means of cutting down dependence on imported oil.

Conversely, the energy industry has something to offer the environment—an advanced, highly sophisticated technology which can be used to ease environmental problems while it seeks solutions to the energy shortage.

Environmentalists have usually looked skeptically at technical solutions, but they are coming to realize that in a highly industrialized, complex society, technology must be used to help nature restore itself.

Since the oil embargo, the interest of the Congress and the Administration and the availability of large sums of money offer an extraordinary opportunity to do energy and environmental research and development together. If the rhetoric can be laid aside, there is much to be done together.

Some efforts contribute directly to the solution of both problems at the same time. For example, our approach to energy conservation is quite primitive. Turning off lights and holding down speed limits save some energy, but they are basically symbols. We are just beginning to research the potential wholesale savings available in the industrial and commercial sectors where 70 percent of the energy is consumed.

There are a wide range of investments in the changing of industrial processes or building practices which may now be economically attractive. We need to know where they are. In some cases, such as a new process now being tested in the aluminum industry, the potential parlay seems almost too good. The system under trial virtually eliminates pollution, cuts electricity costs by 30 percent and reduces operating costs.

Professor Carroll Wilson of the Massachusetts Institute of Technology suggests that the energy costs saved in one year by energy-saving investments could quickly amortize the amount spent to bring about the savings. The cement industry offers a good example. A ton of cement, until recently, cost about $25. Five dollars of this goes for energy. There is presently technology available to lower energy needs by 25 percent or $1.25 per ton. The cost of the change can be amortized in about three years, and thus, for older plants in particular, the change looks like a good energy and profit policy.

Another area of research and development that directly benefits environment and energy is improved design of automobile engines and the development of new alternate fuel sources. The first generation of pollution control devices tried to clean up the internal combustion engine with "add-ons" to the process. These caused fuel penalties that unhappily reached their peak just in time to provoke the unnecessary energy *v.* environment controversy. The second generation of pollution control techniques is now coming on line and their development needs to be pursued.

A third area where energy and environment go hand-in-hand is the development of new or currently little used power systems. Solar energy, geothermal steam, and wind all are free of international power politics and carbon monoxide. None of the three will be a panacea, but each can help. The availability and cost of solar energy is particularly attractive. The point is that the new agents offer a chance to move to practical, widespread use of resources that would otherwise have not been tapped.

Coal is perhaps the most promising in terms of the quantity of energy potentially available. In the past year or so we have rediscovered the vast resources of coal which lie under much of this country. Over the past twenty years we had turned away from coal because much of it was dirty, because it was sometimes dangerous to dig and difficult to handle and because oil cost less than $2 a barrel.

Now there is an opportunity to find ways to process and handle coal in ways that are cleaner and easier. Methods of converting coal into gas or liquid are already known. Work is needed now on how to do it at a reasonable cost and in a way that creates environmentally sound products.

Recycling and resource recovery also save both energy and the environment. It takes only 20 percent as much energy to recycle a ton of aluminum as it does to produce one ton from virgin ore. There are similar energy economies in refining copper and other metals, and, of course, there is the additional saving in the basic metal itself.

There is a very direct environmental-energy benefit in the recycling of garbage. We used to have a solid waste crisis in cities that were running out of landfill sites or places to incinerate the 5½ pounds of garbage each American churns out every day. Now we are beginning to eye that garbage greedily; for it contains the energy value of low-grade coal. St. Louis and other cities are now generating power from garbage and as technology improves, the idea will doubtless spread.

In addition to these efforts, which directly help solve both environmental and energy problems, there are other research and development investments which can ameliorate the adverse impact of energy on the environment and make new energy sources acceptable. Coal, because of its abundance, is a very attractive possibility. At the time the decision was made in the early 1960s, it seemed easier and cheaper to switch to low-sulphur oil rather than trying to take the sulphur out of coal. Desulphurization of coal is presently done by stack gas cleaning, although there is argument about costs, reliability and disposal of residues. A modest development investment here might pay very big clean-energy dividends. Other systems to take the sulphur out before burning may also be feasible.

Other areas in which new technology may lessen the impact of energy production are these: protection of offshore oil drilling operations; restoration of strip-mined land and disposal of nuclear wastes from generators. In these cases the troublesome impacts of energy production might be made more acceptable by the investment of some of the brains and money that now seem to be available.

In Europe, for example, new, low-cost, "Habitat"-type housing is being built on stripped land. Roads, artificial lakes, and open space are being designed to ameliorate the impact of the new contours. Elsewhere, the possibility of starting vineyards on the coal-created terraces is being studied.

There will continue to be conflicts between energy and environment. Technology, no matter how generously funded or imaginatively applied, cannot solve them all. Political science will have to take over where the physical sciences leave off.

But the threat of embargo and the higher prices have brought about a surge of interest and dollars for research and development. This presents a great opportunity. Any partnership that, at the same time, saves oil, reduces the threat to national security, cuts the trade deficit, promotes health, and respects the environment would seem to have a bright future indeed.

VII

The Most Fruitful Use of Our Land

William K. Reilly and John H. Noble

An energy crisis, an economic recession, and a world food shortage have occurred during the three years since publication of *The Use of Land*, the report of the Rockefeller Task Force on Land Use and Urban Growth.[1] All of these have altered to some degree our perceptions of critical land use problems. Very useful analyses could be prepared assessing the relationships between land use and energy,[2] and exploring land use in the United States as it relates to food production.

The Use of Land focused primarily on land for development and land for conservation, and it looked closely into popular attitudes, legal and planning issues, constitutional impediments to land conservation, accounting practices in the development profession, and it included suggestions for both official and citizen responses to land use concerns. Now two years later, where do we stand? What of the best known finding of the Task Force, the existence of a powerful "new mood in America" that questions traditional assumptions about the desirability of urban development? What of the environmental "movement" whose successes in pollution control prompted the Task Force to express confidence that significant new energies might be brought to bear on the more resistant and complex field of land use? What is the relevance of the Task Force's call for national land use policy legislation and for new state laws now that government programs are widely disparaged and public funds much more limited by popular resistance to taxes and bond issues?

Two Years Later: Where Do We Stand Today?

Values: In a Time of Recession and Doubts, the
"New Mood" Apparently Presists

The two years since publication of *The Use of Land* have seen powerful constraints applied to urban development. These have not been principally the intentional constraints—such as protecting critical environmental areas—called for by the "new mood" in its demands for preservation and creation of quality. They have been constraints of quite another kind. The first threatened constraint was energy, for the oil embargo began only a month after the report's publication. The second has been economic, for the bottom fell out of the construction industry not long thereafter.

The Task Force's heralded new mood, which it saw as broadening our national awareness of the objectives served by the human habitat, must now be reappraised in light of rediscovered constraints. For the motivation behind the new mood, concluded the Task Force, "is not exclusively economic. It appears to be a part of a rising emphasis on human values, on the preservation of natural and cultural characteristics that make for a humanly satisfying living environment."[3]

In its assessment of the new mood, the report was on balance optimistic. This new mood was seen to represent a force of great energy. On the one hand it presented a new opportunity: finally, a broad, popular concern for planning and regulating land use had emerged that could be offset against the one-sided, purely economic values that have characterized much development pressure. On the other hand, it presented a challenge, for it encompassed a range of negative attitudes that were acknowledged as "sometimes confused and even hostile to the needs of our society for new development."[4]

Nevertheless, the new mood was judged a "most hopeful portent." Although, concededly, it expressed a range of anxieties and discontents, it nevertheless was regarded as a lever with which changes in land use planning and control could be achieved to make possible a qualitatively different future for Americans.

The spirit and successes of the early environmental "movement" prompted much of this hope of the Task Force on Land Use and Urban Growth. In 1973 the energies of the environmental movement were fresh and powerful and its victories impressive. If those energies could be focused on the problems of land use and urban growth with the same persistence and sophistication that had characterized pollution battles, said the Task Force, the results would potentially be significant.

The Use of Land did not, however, respond to every environmental demand, nor was its tone perfectly congruent with every aspect of the "movement." One journal recently observed that the report "was praised by some environmental groups ... but it was damned by a few, because it concerned itself more with channeling money into 'quality' development, than with banning development entirely."[5] Properly so, for the Task Force recognized the inevitability of urban growth to serve a growing, changing national population. It saw its goal as one of accommodating needed growth without sacrifice of environmental and cultural objectives.

Having established this goal, the Task Force devoted most of its energies to exploring ways to achieve it. What were the opportunities, it asked, to transform new public attitudes into action? What methods should be used? And who should use them? It was these issues of methods and institutions that the Task Force saw as critical and that its report principally addressed.

The explosive entrance upon the scene of the "energy crisis" seemed likely at first to revolutionize development planning and growth patterns: sprawl would stop; careful calculation of the energy costs of building and operating housing would come to dominate siting and density even more surely than infrastructure costs or local fiscal impact analyses; "Homeramas" would darken their blinking lights, depriving families of a major source of weekend recreation.

A few ecologists and others alarmed by our burning of fossil fuels welcomed the constraint. Many more people bewailed the advent of "no-growth." In retrospect it seems that neither celebration nor desperation was in order. Energy limits, notably in the form of higher costs, of course affect development. But there is no evidence yet that energy will soon radically constrain urban life.

The recession, of course, has had devastating impact. The problems are all too familiar: inflating costs for building materials, labor, energy; inflated interest costs even when financing is available; limited consumer ability to buy homes even when people are confident enough to try. The fall-off in housing starts since 1973 has been radical. The prices of existing homes in metropolitan Washington are said to be rising as much as one thousand dollars a month. And as many as 80 percent of the people cannot afford to buy new single-family homes.

Three years of economic and energy constraints—felt not only by the construction industry, of course, but by the whole economy and society—have created uncertainty and uneasiness about future growth. The world view of 1976 is more somber, less confident, perhaps even apprehensive about the future. Nations which doubt their capacity to guarantee supplies of fuel sufficient to heat homes or to enable people to drive to work; economies which perversely persist in inflating prices and unemploying millions—these conditions afflict the developed world, undermining optimism and a sense of efficacy.

The discouragement of 1976, then, much more than the expanded awareness represented by the "new mood," has pressed upon us the prospect of an "era of scarcity" in which resource limitations may indeed have to be recognized.

To many Americans, however, public officials as well as private citizens, constraint remains simply uncongenial, out of keeping with too many customs. Consider energy. Americans certainly do not behave as if this much-discussed constraint constrains them very much. Even when the constraint is thrust upon people immediately, visually—as in lines at gas stations—and relentlessly—as in soaring monthly utility bills and climbing prices at the pump—we avoid responding, we resist acknowledging the consequences. Old values persist in shaping reactions to new situations. At the level of the man in the street, there seems to be little urgency, or even interest, in personal energy conservation. That energy consumption diminished may be attributed to economic recession, not to any new conservation ethic among our people. About less visible problems—the relationship between world hunger and our habit of urbanizing prime agricultural lands, for example—there is little more than a murmur of discussion, nothing like full policy debate or program implementation.

Our national discomfort in thinking about constraints is suggested by the curious and unfortunate absence of a common language to discuss them. There are environmental constraints, and there are economic/political constraints. Each type has its band of champions who dispute the champions of the other type. The environmentalist urging respect for aquifers or earthquakes is too often unconcerned about the dollar costs of environmental constraints—and mistrustful of the developer who urges that economic constraints, too, be considered. By the same token, the developer or businessman familiar with economic and political constraints is far too ready to dismiss out of hand the environmentalist who expresses concern about depletion of fossil fuel supplies or wildlife habitat, not to mention possible damage to the ozone layer. The different values of economics and ecology are reflected in distinct languages without translations.

An even more fundamental difficulty in injecting concern about constraints into the national consciousness arises because not nearly enough is known about them and about the impact that they are likely to have and should have. In most places, environmental constraints do not now appear to be the unavoidable "limits to growth" that they were once perceived to be by some observers. But what should be their impact? Should they wholly reshape development other than at the margins, at those readily identifiable fringe areas where there are high ecological stakes? How confidently do studies of "carrying capacity" and the like enable us to answer this question?

Energy seems a formidable constraint, in the long run if not in the short. Even so, what is the likelihood that energy supply—either in its present form as a political/economic constraint or in the longer run as an ecological one—will stunt the nation's productive capacities? Or will it spur the invention of new technologies? And if so, what help will they be in solving urban needs? Past technological "fixes" have been notably disappointing in the field of housing development.

In short, the front-page constraints—what is known of them today and what is acknowledged about their consequences—do not simplify the job of urban growth management. Now that "energy crisis" discussion has quieted, America does not appear to be on the verge of encountering a radical constraint that will form our cities like the defensive walls of medieval towns. As for the recession, it may disrupt or delay the development process, but it hardly simplifies the achievement of quality in the development that does occur.

Have recession and new concerns about scarcity ended the "new mood," even turned aside the quest for quality? Was the emphasis on human and natural values just a brief historical aberration, a temporary excess associated with the years when the "movement" was riding high? Some people hoped, and still undoubtedly do, that a good stiff recession would flush this quality nonsense out of people's systems once and for all. But public dedication to quality has apparently survived the test: if there is a message in Potomac Associates' most recent testing of the waters, *State of the Nation 1974*,[6] it is that Americans are preoccupied as never before with issues of the environment and the domestic quality of life.

So far at least, available evidence suggests that our society has enlarged its priorities, embracing the environmentalists' concerns. A survey conducted in August 1975 by Opinion Research Corporation, of Princeton, New Jersey, reveals that "Even during a time of recession, high unemployment, and rising fuel costs, the public does not voice a readiness to cut back on environmental control programs to solve economic and energy problems. In fact, six people in ten say that it is important to pay the price necessary to protect the environment." Interpreting this finding the pollsters counsel that "business seems to have little recourse but to learn to cope with and even capitalize on, if at all possible in the long run, the transformation of environmental protection into a popular institutionalized movement which shows little sign of abating even during a period of economic stress."[7] The debate over "quality of life" has become woven into Americans' expectations. Recession may postpone demands for quality, but it cannot defer them indefinitely. This is not an easy time to address issues of quality, to be sure—but to forget it entirely, to be lulled into thinking of quality as a luxury item, would be to misread the last two years.

We must be careful not to overstate the case. The public wants a lot of things, of which "quality" is only one. The past two years have made it even clearer than before that people's expectations are often unrealistically high and even contradictory. Government is expected to be efficient, prompt, responsive, and strong in correcting maldistribution of wealth, deterring sprawl, in protecting scenic coasts from pollution, in providing comfortable and efficient public transportation, in thwarting intrusive or disfiguring highrises. At the same time, it had better consult with every affected interest, it must not interfere with the individual's right to drive an automobile, or to own a single-family dwelling, or perhaps even to build a resort cottage.

In short, the quality values of the "new mood" persist—but so do the powerful consumption drives that antedate it and that recession has not dampened. The opportunity represented by the "new mood" remains, but so does the problem of finding practical ways to reconcile conflicting expectations. All the choices we make must ultimately contribute to solution of this problem.

Protecting What We Value: Both the states and the federal government have taken on additional responsibilities for protecting critical environmental areas. The issues are whether their actions are effective and whether they should do still more.

One essential for the improved land use sought by the Task Force is "protecting what we value." This element responds to the planner's traditional recognition of the need for green spaces in healthy communities, both for recreation and visual enjoyment; the historic preservationist's sensitivity to a rich endowment of architecture in the built environment; the conservationist's concern for wilderness, for unique and beautiful habitats; and the environmentalist's identification of ecosystems crucial to the maintenance of life, and of areas needed to moderate or buffer the forces of nature.

To protect open space assets, the report recommended a mix of measures, including land acquisition, several sorts of regulations, tax incentives, and sensitive adaptation of governmental construction programs to open space needs. It gave high priority to public acquisition of recreation lands. Especially in newly urbanizing areas, both recreation and social needs were said to be best served by establishing as public policy that the limited natural supply of prime recreational open spaces, particularly beaches and other waterfront areas, should, to the maximum feasible extent, be acquired by government, preserved, and made publicly accessible. Federal spending for open space acquisition was defended and both federal and state governments were urged to adjust open space acquisition plans to rising needs.

Yet acquisition was deemed insufficient and inappropriate to protect all worthy open spaces. Since it is neither feasible nor acceptable for governments to acquire the vast agricultural and natural areas that ought to be conserved within future urban regions, mechanisms to protect privately held open space are essential. Without such mechanisms, even moderate objectives of protection programs are unlikely to be achieved.

Among the several measures recommended to protect privately owned open spaces, the report laid special emphasis on regulations. To supplement local actions it called for state regulations and federal support and assistance, asking state as well as local governments to establish protective regulations to prevent development that would be incompatible with open space needs in critical agricultural and environmental areas. Where protected areas are carefully selected through comprehensive planning, states were urged to authorize and encourage in appropriate cases, very low density zoning, including, for example, requirements for fifty or more acres per dwelling unit. Enactment of pending national land use policy legislation was strongly endorsed.

A mix of techniques—including public acquisition of land and of development rights in strategic land parcels (those located along highways, directly adjoining urbanized areas, and along waterfronts) but with primary reliance on federally supported, state-administered, noncompensatory regulations—appeared then to present the only realistic hope of achieving the permanent protection of critical open spaces, including buffer zones between urbanized areas.

Turning to the cities, where the problems of protection from development are different—the assets are human, not natural—but no less intractable than in the countryside, the Task Force took up historic preservation. It pushed hard for a broader set of criteria for recognizing sites worthy of designation in The National Register of Historic Places, so that "urban neighborhoods characterized by a mix of uses, a vitality of street life, and a physical integrity" could qualify as "conservation areas."[8] "For historic preservation, as for open space protection," the Task Force concluded, "the first requisite is a framework for regulation, preferably a statewide system for registration of historic districts and properties and a clear policy favoring preservation."[9]

Just as the feasibility of protection was said to depend significantly upon regulations, so the feasibility of regulations was said to depend upon the willingness of elected officials to enact them and of judges to uphold them. To make needed regulations feasible, the report concluded, changed public attitudes toward land are essential.

Historically, Americans have thought of urbanization rights as coming from the land itself, "up from the bottom," like minerals or crops. It is equally possible to view them as coming "down from the top," as being created by society and allocated by it to each land parcel. The Task Force declared: "We think it highly likely that in forthcoming decades Americans will gradually abandon the traditional assumption that urbanization rights arise from the land itself. Development potential, on any land and in any community, results largely from the actions of society (especially the construction of public facilities)."[10]

In its most controversial recommendations, the report also called for reexamination of judicial precedent governing the validity of highly restrictive regulations. To protect critical environmental and cultural areas, the Task Force said, "tough restrictions will have to be placed on the use of privately owned land. These restrictions will be little more than delaying actions if the courts do not uphold them as reasonable measures to protect the public interest, in short, as restrictions that landowners may fairly be required to bear without payment by the government. The interpretation of the "takings clause" (which has sometimes been construed to prohibit governmental restrictions on the use of privately-owned land as, in effect, "takings" of the land itself for which landowners must be compensated) is therefore a crucial matter for future land use planning and regulatory programs.

"Many judicial precedents, including some from the U.S. Supreme Court, date from a time when attitudes toward land, natural processes, and planning were different than they are today. Many precedents are anachronistic now that land is coming to be regarded as a basic natural resource to be protected and conserved and urban development is seen as a process needing careful public guidance and control."[11]

In recommending acquisition, regulations, and other measures to protect critical areas and other open spaces, *The Use of Land* stressed the need for action by governments at every level: local, state, federal. The report placed particular emphasis, however, on state regulations. In a field traditionally dominated by local governments, proposals to shift some responsibilities elsewhere raise key issues.

The Expanded State Role. As *The Use of Land* recognized, local governments are not at all likely to fade out of the land use guidance picture. Indeed, local governments will almost surely continue to make most of the decisions that form the guidance process. No other government is usually better qualified to make most of these decisions, if only because there are so many of them and because each needs to respond to so many conditions (natural, cultural, economic, social) that vary greatly from place to place.

Still, many observers of American land use and of the guidance process have for years expressed dissatisfaction with local performance, not just in protecting critical areas but in the whole range of land use responsibilities:

1. Many localities choose to take little or no effective action to guide land use within their boundaries.
2. Other localities are unable to act effectively because they are small, impoverished, understaffed, corrupt, or for any number of other reasons.
3. Some localities use their land use powers to exclude unpopular but needed development (e.g., homes for low-income families).

In response to such problems as these, some observers have long advocated a shift of some land use guidance powers to other levels of government. At one time, their emphasis was on creating new governments at the metropolitan level. And there have been continuing efforts to increase the influence of metropolitan and regional planning entities. Throughout the 1970s, however, the greatest interest has focused on encouraging the states to exercise more of the powers that they have traditionally delegated to their localities.

In calling for greater reliance on state action to protect open spaces, the Task Force allied itself with this approach. Experience during the past two years has brought scores of state statutes consistent with the Task Force's recommended approach. Any effort to compile state actions protecting wetlands, beaches, the coastal zone, and other key areas is destined to be obsolete within weeks after its preparation. Nothing now visible suggests that this surge of state protective action will soon fade.

There remain many unanswered questions about state protective actions. Exactly how, for instance, can a state best divide protective responsibility between itself and its localities? Should local rules prevail if they are tougher than the state rules? Should state rules apply everywhere, or only in localities that don't have their own protective rules or staffs capable of enforcing them? How should the state respond to the presence of highly qualified staffs in some localities, perhaps more qualified than the state staff? These questions, however, and the many more like them, are essentially details within the context of expanded state protective responsibility. That context had been established by 1973, and it is even more clearly established today.

The Federal Role: Also Expanded But Without a Land-Use Act. Like the states, the federal government is taking important actions to protect critical areas and other open spaces. Some of these actions preceded *The Use of Land*; others are more recent. Some operate upon or through the state; others do not. Among the noteworthy federal actions are these:

1. The environmental impact statement requirement of the National Environmental Policy Act.
2. Section 208 of the 1972 Water Pollution Control Act Amendments, which has far-reaching implications for land planning and regulation.
3. Section 404 of the same act, which provides the statutory basis for Corps of Engineers regulations that have great promise as protectors of wetlands.
4. The Coastal Zone Management programs for coastal areas, including attention to critical areas.
5. The Flood Disaster Protection Act of 1973, with its federal land-use policies and tough funding-cutoff implementation requirements.

Many of these laws are still so recent that their full impact—like that of many comparable state laws—is not yet clear. As implementation efforts proceed, their effectiveness will need to be continually evaluated. It is premature to predict the outcome of those evaluations.

It is worth noting, nevertheless, that these environmental laws could yet produce a period of disenchantment. Ten years hence, it is conceivable that we may regard 1969 to 1974 as a brief period of agreement on means for dealing with perceived environmental threats, just as 1964 to 1968 now seems to have been a moment of temporary national consensus on attempts to deal with poverty. The years following each period of commitment might then be seen as the difficult time of realizing that consensus on means does not translate into unanimity about ends, that enacting a law to keep flood plains free of obstruction or to hold forth a goal of swimmable water everywhere is quite different from enforcing it once its full costs are known. That is, environmental laws and programs that now carry the look of winners could undergo a period of reassessment like the one that the poverty programs of the 1960s are now experiencing.

Environmental advocates may then derive from a similar period of skepticism lessons surprisingly like those now surrounding our urban experience. Chief among them might be a conclusion that some types of federal action tend to work better than others—and that federal action cannot really achieve a lot of what needs to be done.

Despite the numerous actions that the federal government has taken to protect critical areas and other open spaces, a good deal more attention has been focused on actions that it has *not* taken. Specifically, it has *not* enacted a national land use policy or planning assistance act. The Task Force "urgently" recommended enactment of such legislation as a means "to encourage state and local regulation in a balanced framework that is respectful both of conservation and development priorities."[12]

Several bills of the type recommended by the Task Force have been considered by the Congress in recent years. These bills have been quite unlike federal air and water quality legislation. That legislation establishes substantive federal goals (e.g., water safe for shellfish production and swimming by 1983, zero discharge of pollutants by 1985), and establishes precise standards and elaborate requirements, procedures, and timetables for achieving them. The thrust of the land use bills has been quite different—much more like that of the Coastal Zone Management Act. They would give land use a federal imprimatur as a matter of national concern, and they would pump in federal funds. Some would also have provided for modest federal standards, particularly aimed at discouraging development of prime agricultural lands. All would have established federal terminology and a federal context for continuing experimentation by state and local governments.

Even after enactment of any such bills, however, states and localities would continue to play a far more creative, decisive role in land use than many of them do in achieving air or water quality. Indeed, the main thrust of federal land use bills has been toward a larger role for the states—and *not* under terms that would turn the affected state agency into a sort of subcontractor hired to achieve federal goals.

How useful would such legislation be? What impact should we expect of it a few years after enactment? Some Washington observers find these issues moot, at least temporarily, for want of political interest in this type of legislation. They may or may not be correct. Still, the issue remains: should such legislation be receiving priority attention as recommended two years ago by the Task Force?

Support for this legislative approach appears to remain strong among thoughtful professionals concerned with growth management. At a small, national land use conference sponsored early in 1975 by The Conservation

Foundation, there was great interest in this approach as one that would strengthen state efforts to integrate many individual programs concerned with development and protection. Planners saw the bills as creating an opportunity to achieve something closer to comprehensiveness, to coordinate programs that are now disparate. There was consensus that many states would spend federal land use planning grants wisely and that, despite some predictable waste, such a program would be beneficial.

At least a few environmentalists, however, have questioned the desirability of this type of legislation. Their concern may stem from something elusive about the very concept of "land use." Wise use of land, it turns out, is often not much easier to agree upon than wise use of money. Either can be stated as a goal, but neither—unlike a goal of "clean water"—can serve as a touchstone later when disagreement arises about how to achieve it. Without more articulation or an unstated agreement about what it really means, a policy of "wise land use" amounts to little more than a policy of working out disputes later, under, perhaps, some agreed-to process.

This difficulty may contribute to the apparent failure of land use legislation to stir some citizen environmentalists who are fully committed to clean water, or to the protection of wilderness or wetlands. Some fear that the state programs aided by the legislation could prove to be "anti-environmental," favoring development of some sites that citizens or local governments find environmentally significant. Others are merely uncertain of what the state programs might produce. And some suspect that state agencies would be less protection-oriented than local governments newly responsive to the "new mood."

Uncertainty about likely impact appears also to have generated some of the intense opposition that this legislative approach has experienced in Congress. Even if a builder or landowner does not welcome a federal ban on houses in floodways, for example, he is at least aware that floods are a problem and that the ban responds to that problem. When he hears only of "land use" legislation he may wonder just what the specific purpose will turn out to be. At a Conservation Foundation conference for state representatives one legislator made the point in roughly these terms:

The people in my district are ready for floodplain regulations. They know it's stupid to build houses where the owners get flooded out every now and then and have to be rescued in small boats. So I can probably sell a program called "floodplain conservation" or something like that. But I sure don't want to try to sell something called "land use" because the first thing they think of then is somebody from the state capital coming down and telling them what they can't do on their own farm.

Some may infer from all this that the federal government could do more to protect critical areas and other open spaces by turning away from a general or comprehensive approach and relying exclusively on more narrowly focused federal statutes and state-assistance programs.

Others might instead conclude that the land use bills should not be viewed principally as environmental legislation focusing on protection of critical areas. Rather, they should rise or fall as planning bills, concerned with comprehensiveness and coordination of programs. So viewed, the bills respond to traditional concerns of planners. But those concerns include not just the preservation of quality, but also its creation, and the legislative approach must accordingly be judged within that much larger and more complicated context.

Creating Quality in Development: The unfolding new mood focuses more clearly on participatory democracy, with important implications both for defining quality and for achieving it.

A principal concern of the Task Force was creating quality in new development. Despite the difficulty of achieving protection objectives, the obstacles to creation of quality proved even more formidable:

It is harder to create quality then to preserve it, for creation requires more choices and its goals are inherently complicated. In conservation, quality values are readily translated into physical ideals and, in many cases, the ideals already exist—a community in harmony with its surroundings, a valley preserved in wilderness.

If the community or valley is instead to be transformed by development, there are no such convenient ideals. At what population level is there likely to be the greatest concern for the humanity of each inhabitant? Is it better that people live close together or far apart? That they walk to work, drive, be carried by mass transit, or perhaps by elevator within a futuristic megastructure? How much social contact should we aim for among people of different temperaments, incomes, races, and ethnic backgrounds?

No consensus exists on these issues, and none is likely to be forthcoming soon. A consensus may someday arise, most likely from a better understanding of the natural constraints on development . . . and the innate needs of human beings and societies, but for the foreseeable future, the decisions that create and shape our communities and regions will continue to be made without ideal development patterns, social or physical.[13]

Without consensus, measures intended to create quality must cope as best they can with inevitable tension between the whole of a community and its parts. Quality, when created as when preserved, requires harmony among whole and parts, although both continually change as parts are built and altered and destroyed. A customary task of planners is to assure that each new part respects the whole—and not just the whole that exists but also the whole that should exist and could exist. A customary problem of planners is that their vision of the whole can never be complete, since it must depend on the parts—again not just those that exist but those that should exist and could exist.

Facing this dilemma, the Task Force recommended quality-creating measures that are less concrete than the measures it recommended for protection. It recommended use of both regulations and incentives. It noted the discouraging experience with regulations. Traditional zoning controls rely on a legislated vision of the whole community and require future parts to conform to it; these controls are at least as unsatisfactory as the vision on which they rest. Yet the principal alternative—focusing the regulatory process on a particular bit of proposed construction and evaluating it by applying standards that are typically very general (if they exist at all)—also often leads to unsound decisions coupled with charges of incompetence, conflict of interest, "ad hockery," even corruption.

The Task Force nevertheless concluded that the latter, development-focused alternative holds greater potential for sound, fair decisions. It pointed to environmental impact analysis as a sound technique of this type:

The best regulatory mechanism so far for development review is environmental impact analysis. The great benefits of the process are its focus on proposed development, its consideration of feasible alternatives, and its . . . concept of seeking among feasible alternatives what is best for the public interest.[14]

Safeguards must be established, however, to increase the likelihood that the process will work effectively and fairly. There must be a sound process of planning and policy-making and simplified processing for small projects, and conflict of interest regulations. The Task Force placed greatest emphasis, however, on measures to facilitate citizen involvement in the process:

Every element of the regulatory process, including deliberations, advisory recommendations, and final decisions, should take place at advertised meetings open to the public. Local and state laws should establish open meeting requirements for all governmental agencies responsible for land-use regulations.[15]

Citizen suits appealing from local regulatory decisions should be permitted by any local resident or civic organization in the public interest, without regard to property ownership or other financial interest.[16]

Also, the regulating government must be large enough to represent all those principally affected by the proposed development:

Important development should be regulated by governments that represent all the people whose lives are likely to be affected by it, including those who could benefit from it as well as those who could be harmed by it. Where a regulatory decision significantly affects people in more than one locality, state, regional, or even federal action is necessary.

Congress should enact a national land-use policy act authorizing federal funding for states to assert control over land use of state or regional impact and concern.[17]

Despite its conclusion that reliance on regulations is inevitable, the Task Force recognized that regulations can, at best, do only part of the job of creating quality—and probably not the most important part.

Even though communities must be more effectively protected against inappropriate development, additional protection is not the most pressing need at the community level. The greater need is to remold the development process—not only the regulatory process but also the methods by which land and utilities are made available—in order to foster quality development.[18]

We have consciously focused less on negative compulsion than on creating positive inducements. . . .[19]

But what methods could be used to create those positive inducements? The Task Force saw some potential contribution from environmental impact analysis:

In the long run, the greatest importance of the environmental impact analysis process may lie in its establishment of a higher standard of conduct for development agencies, requiring them to publicly evaluate opportunities within a broad spectrum of public objectives.[20]

It also recommended a number of measures to enlarge the scale of development. "Although an increase in scale does not guarantee higher quality, it significantly increases the developer's opportunity to achieve quality."[21] This is true, the Task Force concluded, because the large project provides enough maneuvering room for flexibility in design, a budget large enough to support professional design staff, and often a long-term involvement with the project that creates incentives to provide lasting quality.

But the Task Force recognized that still other approaches remain to be devised, publicly and privately, to establish sufficient incentives for quality. It put the goal this way:

The development process should, insofar as possible, be shaped by planning and regulatory bodies, lenders, accountants, appraisers, and other participants so that developers, home-buyers, and other consumers come to perceive the maintenance and enhancement of quality as the key to profitability. Divergence between quality and profitability should be minimized.[22]

There was, and is, a long way to go to carry out that principle. In examining the experience of the two years since the report was released, any movement toward measures that create quality deserves our particular attention. As we will now see, most of that experience does not provide answers, but only exposes new facets of the questions.

In choosing processes, rather than substantive standards, as the greater hope for achieving quality in development, *The Use of Land* recognized the need for safeguards to make the chosen processes work soundly and fairly. Among the recommended safeguards, as we have seen, it stressed opportunities for citizen involvement. The Task Force thus responded to an important element of the new mood: the demand for direct participation by individuals in the decisions that affect their lives.

Now, two years later, this participatory element of the new mood appears even more emphatic. Mistrust of the governmental institutions traditionally responsible for satisfying people's demands appears to have grown; it certainly has become more widely articulated. So has the consequent insistence on a more direct popular voice in decision-making, not just on growth-related issues but on many others as well.

The intensifying mistrust of governmental institutions has two dimensions. The enactment of new laws, the creation of new institutions, and the expenditure of vast amounts of funds to solve problems that persist and in some cases—crime, for example—even worsen, have made people doubt the *capacity* of government. Extravagant claims for governmental performance, excessively optimistic prognoses by government leaders, opportunistic management of the economy for political gains, deceptive and illegal federal actions, have made people doubt the *integrity* of government.

This sudden reaction against government—a shift in attitudes making the familiar seem strange, the well-meaning alien—is much more than a response to uniquely American problems such as Watergate. The same phenomenon, hitting with particular force those parts of the public sector concerned with land use and development issues, seems to be occurring in every developed country. Even in nations where there is no tradition of nongovernmental participation in decision-making—France, Germany, Japan—public dissent over official development schemes is reaching epidemic levels.

Government responses range from the incredulous, to the cynical, to the imaginative.

1. In Germany some local governments are handling public protest against official proposals by offering residents a referendum on three development choices, the least intrusive of which voters can be depended on to select and acquiesce in. It will typically be less large than the government's initial proposal, but far bigger than what local residents would really prefer.
2. In the Netherlands the government takes an open, helpful attitude towards protest groups, even subsidizing them. According to some observers, this works like sugar with horses and one sometimes ends up with gilded geldings prancing on a string.
3. In Japan the government Development Bank has declined to make loans for projects unless the local governments in which they are proposed actually invest and assume an equity position in the projects. Apparently, the town fathers won't put their money on a clearly unpopular project, and once their

money is in they can be counted on to put all their weight behind getting it built.
4. In France the President of the Republic, in response to public protest, has
   effectively repudiated M. Pompidou's famous dictum about the task lying
   before Paris being to adapt the city to the automobile. His bureaucracy is a
   long way from getting the message, however.
5. In Australia trade unions have imposed "green bans" against the demolition
   of historic or locally valued developments. In the spring of 1975, such
   refusals to work on unpopular redevelopment schemes had stopped over four
   billion Australian dollars in development projects.

Part of this revulsion against customary ways is pervasive disappointment
with the fruits of "expertise," an almost anarchic reaction discounting the
ability of professionals to achieve desired ends. In London, Amsterdam, Munich,
Paris, Sydney, and Tokyo, as in so many American cities, public officials and
professionals have been busy during the post-World War II period constructing a
built environment that ordinary people now perceive does not work. Around the
world urban residents are coming to view themselves as the victims, not the
beneficiaries of urban change, change that results in large and intrusive buildings
and developments, change that disrupts and uproots. And increasingly people are
uniting in opposition to it. This feeling is negative, borne of opposition, of
unwillingness to let "them" do something—"get away with it"—the consequences of which are disliked. Even this negativism has its value, for without
consensus on quality development, listening to what people do *not* want often
provides the best available—though still imperfect—guide to their unexpressed
wants and needs.

And there is another aspect that is positive and creative. It values participation and control, the rediscovery of personal capabilities, and the accompanying
sense of autonomy. In the words of Colin Ward,

We are groping for a different political theory and for a different aesthetic
theory. The missing political element is the politics of participation. The missing
cultural element is the aesthetic of a variable, manipulable, malleable environment, an environment of "loose parts," [in which, (according to Simon
Nicholson who evolved the concept)] "both the degree of inventiveness and
creativity and the possibility of discovery, are directly proportional to the
number and kind of variables in it."[23]

In place of the environment designed, built, and imposed by elected officials
and trained professionals, we are seeing indigenous proposals and counterpro-
posals. In place of the "long democracy"—whereby local elected officials could
count on making decisions more or less on their own and consulting the people
in elections every two or four years—we now see "short democracy" in which
urban residents expect to be consulted about most important decisions. The new

era we have entered may be accepted or fought, but it should be recognized as a positive force for conserving cities. Writing nearly a century ago, Charles Peguy offered this warning:

A society which offers to the descendants of those who built our cathedrals no other function than, at best, to be their caretakers, should not be surprised if some of them, for sheer distraction, end by smashing the windows.[24]

We live in a time when too many people feel like breaking the windows of the cathedrals, when too many people feel threatened by change, and when the legitimacy of governmental institutions—and of many other sources of authority as well, such as churches, schools, corporations and labor unions—is in question. As society has treated people only like consumers, so they have lost faith in their power to shape their own destiny, or to contribute positively to their society. Now they are demanding to do more than consume. At its best, the demand for participation is a demand to shape their worlds, not just to partake passively of what is offered to them.

Although we shall see that this democratic unfolding of the new mood brings problems as well as benefits, it is clearly a significant force and apparently also a growing one. It appears to confirm some elements of the quality-creating processes envisioned in *The Use of Land*, but it draws others into question. And it will pose a couple of critical issues in our future.

The Scale of Government: Is Bigger Better? Since the early 1950s, searchers for improved growth management have commonly issued a prescription that might irreverently be titled: bigger is better. Given the demonstrated inadequacies of growth management by local governments, the reasoning runs, maybe states or regions or the federal government can do better. As we have seen, *The Use of Land* applied this reasoning in its recommendation of state and federal action to protect critical areas and other open spaces.

On the developmental side, too, the report advocated increased responsibility for larger governments. Although "the broad base of regulations should be established by local decisions," the report recommends "a number of measures to inject higher levels of government into the development guidance process."[25] If local governments are too small to represent all the people affected by their decisions, the states should intervene. "States may choose to intervene either to provide additional protection—as we recommend for protection of open spaces and historic properties—or to provide development opportunity where local regulations are too restrictive."[26] Such intervention might be needed to override local regulations that disregard regional needs—by excluding low- and moderate-income housing, for example.

A usual corollary of the "bigger is better" approach has been professionalism. This amounts to an assertion that formal analysis, planning, and policy-making are needed to cope maturely with complex regional problems—and a further assertion that these intricate processes require time and expertise that full-time professionals can best provide.

The unfolding of the new mood reveals intensifying counterforces to the "bigger is better" approach. When government in general is mistrusted, proposals that public officials more "remote" from the scene of local conflicts be given a say in them, seem to many to be headed in precisely the wrong direction. Indeed, a good deal of the current urban excitement is taking place in areas even smaller than local governments, in inner city neighborhoods. Research that The Conservation Foundation presented at a conference on neighborhood conservation in New York in September 1975 describes the revitalization of Seattle's Pioneer Square and Pike Place Market, of Cincinnati's Mt. Adams and Mount Auburn. A recent Urban Land Institute survey reported instances of this phenomenon across the country, in hundreds of cities, all in face of a skeptical financial community. Should not regulations be locally fashioned to respond to local needs? Is that not the way to achieve the citizen participation that this neighborhood manifestation of the unfolding new mood calls for?

Much of the time, it is. But public participation, important as it is, is not the only objective of growth management. Particularly because of the danger that communities will seek to exclude racial and ethnic minorities, community control must at least be subject to outside review in specific cases. Small-scale community organization presents an opportunity to build quality environments, respectful of local differences, but exclusion is an unacceptable price to pay for it. Exclusion by participating citizens themselves is no more acceptable than exclusion at the behest of their elected representatives.

We would do well to recognize, therefore, that efforts to protect valued localities are, quite properly, judged in part by the perceived "threats" that cause the residents to seek protection. Many of us concerned about growth management are quite comfortable when a neighborhood organizes itself to prevent destruction by a superhighway. The same is true when the threat is replacement of an historic area by highrise office buildings.

Quite the reverse is true, and must remain true, when the "threat" comes from members of another ethnic or racial group who seek to make their homes in the community. These are times when the community's own sense of place must be deliberately overridden in the interests of the larger society. This is true when the exclusive suburb decides to bar all moderate-income housing from its borders. It is equally true when an urban neighborhood organizes to defend itself, not against uprooting by urban renewal or an expressway, but against the members of unwanted racial or ethnic groups.

Finding the delicate balance of government powers is part of the mature sorting out of governmental responsibilities so important to policies for building quality communities. It is a sophisticated, difficult process, requiring us to move beyond simple notions—"let the feds do it," or "that's something for City Hall."

With the added pressures posed by the unfolding of the new mood, the process of selecting which level of government is best equipped to manage growth and improve development quality will continue to present some of the most difficult and important land issues of the near future. Obviously, blind devotion to "bigger is better" will not answer all our questions. Nor are simplistic calls for dismantling higher levels of government control—"bigger is anathema"—sufficient to answer the questions. It seems likely that some plural answers to these questions—many of them now being tested in innovative state legislation, and before the courts—will dominate our attempts to resolve this conflict.

The Scale of Development: What About Bigness There? *The Use of Land* applied the "bigger is better" approach to the private sector just as it did to regulating governments. There it meant that developers would, in place of the small and scattered subdivisions typical in the past, increase the scale of their operations to include planned unit developments and even new towns. On enlarged staffs they could carry professional planners and environmental specialists able to create comprehensive, integrated new developments, anticipating a range of needs and planning appropriate responses. Despite discouraging experience with new towns, the view that bigger *may be* better remains strong in the planning and planning law professions. Certainly, the opportunity for sophisticated urban design can be greater in a large project, not only because of the opportunity for professional involvement but also because traditional land controls are more readily modified for large projects.

New mood demands for participation and community control have created counterpressures to large-scale developments. The object of most criticism directed by mail to the Task Force was the report's treatment of the taking issue; of almost equal concern to the people who wrote letters was the endorsement of large-scale development. People in the environmental community, the League of Women Voters, and community organizations could not fathom how large-scale projects could avoid being intrusive, impersonal, and beyond their control. If anything, this sentiment appears to have quickened.

Unlike the problems of scale in government, disputes over scale of development may not produce significant future conflicts and require significant choices. This is because many private builders are also questioning the "bigger is better" assumptions that they, too, have accepted for a decade and more. Some now say that large projects, being more visible, draw more public fire, compounding already enormous problems of securing approvals from government authorities at the local, state, and federal levels. Their more serious problem, however, is economic. Large projects, with the community and recreational facilities so popular among planners and builders alike until the recent recession, impose huge front-end costs. Yet many builders found that sales of single-family houses, in smaller projects without many facilities, have held up better during the recession. Thus clusters, PUD's, new towns—the very large-scale projects that *The Use of Land* thought desirable to achieve environmental and social goals jointly in managing urban growth—present the most difficult, entangling political and economic burdens of predevelopment planning and preparation. In face of it all, some developers are talking about a return to the bad old days of the 1940s and 50s: small-scale tract development of single-family detached dwellings.

Even if economic forces mean that there will be no difficult future choices to be made between small and large projects, the forcefulness of the protest against large-scale development enhances our understanding of the new mood. If the objective were to achieve quality as defined by top professionals in the field of urban design, large projects—which can provide those designers more maneuvering room—would presumably enjoy considerable appeal. The protest against them thus reinforces the impression that the objective of many new mooders is *not* to cause developers to consult "good" designers, instead of mediocre ones or none at all. What is sought, rather, is the opportunity for private citizens and communities to define quality for themselves and to make that definition stick. For some the value placed on participation in the development decision-making process per se, may come to transcend even the satisfactions derived from the outcomes of that choice. To accommodate this mood, the nation will indeed have to "make peace with pluralism," as the Task Force put it, and accommodate great diversity among individuals and communities.

The Search for Incentives: Any Progress? Has the unfolding of the new mood helped to establish quality-creating incentives, which the Task Force found so important yet so elusive? In the absence of consensus about what constitutes quality, one possible response is to encourage individual diversity, plural paths, maximum choice along the road to improved urban life. If this approach is followed, there is diminished reliance on regulations to achieve quality, with the result that the public necessarily places more of its reliance on incentives.

A forceful advocate of this approach is Sir Keith Joseph, the British Conservative, who shares the Task Force's preference for incentives, coupled—it would seem—with some new mooders' attitudes toward the ability of planners to define quality. He expressed his views in attacking the British planning system—which the Task Force admired—at the "Continuing Heritage" Conference of the Civic Trust of Great Britain and the Royal Institute of British Architects, in July 1975. After recognizing the need for "negative" controls for such purposes as preservation, he turned to efforts to obtain aesthetic quality in new development:

The belief that we can enthrone aesthetic quality as an objective of government policy is a naive myth.... Our heritage is not only of palaces and castles, ... [but also] of churches and farms, of cottages, and market squares, of barns and of town houses reflecting civilized communities for half a millenium.
It was not planning that gave us these things. Yet we recognise their quality

when we use the planning machine of today to conserve the products of the non-planning of the past.

How did they manage to produce such fine buildings without anyone but the architect and the client to impose their own idea of quality? The answer is that side by side with the undeniably excellent, they produced a great deal of mediocrity as well. Later generations have chosen and preserved some of the best; they have destroyed most of the worst. Time has proved to be a better judge of quality than planners.

It is in this sense that what matters is not quality but variety and spontaneity—a rich continuing heritage from which future generations will choose what is of real merit. Quality is a by-product of the uncontrolled, often conflicting, energies of countless individuals. We cannot have it by decree, and even if we could, our descendents might have very different ideas of what was beautiful and what ugly.[27]

He observed that "we have been and are moving faster and faster in the opposite direction—discouraging the small, the untidy, the cheap—encouraging the planned, the large, and the uniform." Current confusion in our own national programs suggests that some modesty may be in order in the Colonies, as well. All the more reason, then, for attending to Sir Keith Joseph's elegant recommendation:

Governments should wherever possible achieve their aims by so organizing laws and taxes as to encourage people to do in their own interest that which is in the public interest. This is the way that a free civilized society should work—with government creating the frame-work within which what people need is spontaneously done.[28]

Given the pluralism of the new mood in the United States, some communities will probably follow Sir Keith Joseph's approach, seeking desired action, correspondingly reducing emphasis on regulatory processes that seek to coerce, at great cost, the right result in every case.

For two reasons, though, we must question whether any such respect for individual choices is likely to be the main thrust of the quest for participatory democracy. First, even if the need for incentives is clear, incentive systems have not often enough demonstrated capability to produce results that the public will find acceptable. Among many citizens, mistrust of developers is great, and for them the need is for more regulation, not less. Incentive strategies, little understood, can unfortunately appear to be a call for the abandonment of government policy rather than a new direction for policy and strategy, as, for example, when a density bonus offered a developer in exchange for special responsiveness to environmental protection appears to be a breach in the planning and regulatory policies of a community.

Second, it is not clear that any likely system of incentives will satisfy the desire for participation. The absence of consensus on quality, although it may lead some communities to defer to individual tastes, is likely to lead others to require conformity to the current taste of community residents. This is not a new problem, of course. It is part of the inevitable tension between community and individual, a tension which local land use regulations in the United States have experienced since their inception. In many communities, the new mood is likely to heighten that tension, thereby producing some of the most difficult land use issues to be faced in the years ahead.

Making the Process Work: Toward
Mediation and Beyond

During the past two years, as the new mood has unfolded, there have been increased pressures to make land use more responsive to community attitudes.

The unfolding new mood thereby intensifies age-old problems of law and government, for community attitudes can be arbitrary and unfair, especially to those inadequately represented in the community, or excluded from it entirely. Demands for community determination can thus clash with individual rights protected by the rule of law, by requirements of regularity instead of arbitrariness, fairness rather than mere representativeness.

Opening the process to public participation generates other difficulties as well, ones that the Task Force recognized. Administrative procedures that grant standing to more interests often take longer to resolve than those that are closed. Regulatory systems of review which inject regional or state perspectives into local land use decisions, or which require preparation of documents on the environmental consequences of development, can be more costly and more time-consuming than informal review of permit applications before a local zoning board. There thus remains a clear need for devices to hold to a minimum incremental costs of additional planning, to reduce delays, and to eliminate duplication.

The major new issue for land use emerging of late, and not addressed by *The Use of Land*, is how to cope with the problems of success. This issue is particularly one of going beyond the adversary processes—so essential when new mood concerns are being callously overridden by powerful adversaries—to the creative processes needed to fashion imaginative solutions after all interests are recognized and accepted as legitimate participants in the decision-making process. In this context, the inadequacy of adversary postures to effect adequate accommodation of multiple interests is increasingly clear.

How does democracy begin to hear and to satisfy myriad interests? The participatory processes that raise this problem to the level of a matter for policy-making concern, promise possible solutions as well. For processes which satisfy participatory demands, often are those which elicit opinion and forge consensus—even if temporary—out of it. Our past indicates that much of the genius of American politics lies precisely in such solutions. After being admitted to the conference table, the new mood should increase its reliance on processes that *build* consensus, rather than continuing to rely on the processes that are our only choice when new mood concerns are denied admittance or even recognition.

The Task Force did not foresee this problem, nor did it attempt to recommend solutions. But the germ of a solution may be appearing amidst the creative turmoil of participation in land use decision-making around the world. The Conservation Foundation's ongoing International Comparative Land Use Program is uncovering and exploring possible processes for conflict resolution. One such mechanism is mediation.

The Ford and Rockefeller Foundations recently funded an Office of Environmental Mediation at the University of Washington. The office will support the continuing work of several mediation experts who have already successfully resolved a years-long dispute over flood control and development of unspoiled areas around the Snoqualmie River in Washington. Mediation is used formally abroad, in the appeals process for planning approvals in England, and in public inquiries. And there are numerous mechanisms and opportunities for informal mediation in domestic land and growth policy processes.

Mediation goes beyond a public right to be heard, as in a public hearing devoted to choosing among predetermined alternatives. Rather it means establishing a single forum in which many divergent interests, each accepted from the outset as legitimate, participate in seeking consensus. Mediation does not squeeze multifaceted problems onto a two-sided forum. The final solution may diverge considerably from what any of the parties had in mind at the outset. The very opportunity for participation in this sort of forum often makes people more amenable to—even committed to—changes made necessary by development.

We already indulge in this sort of process, in "consultations" which so often accompany zoning proceedings. The trouble is that our fondness for formal, public adversary procedure is preventing us from seeing what is happening. Until we recognize the phenomenon, we cannot address it and build in essential safeguards to ensure the compatibility of mediated solutions with the protection of rights under law.

A call for broader participation may seem out of step with the Supreme Court's recent holding in *Warth* v. *Seldin*, which upheld suburban land use plans against charges by center city residents and others that they were unconstitutionally exclusionary. Were *Warth* to be interpreted to mean that only a few narrow and immediate interests should be considered in resolving urban growth issues, then of course any call for broader representation of interests would be out of step. If it instead is read to mean that the courts recognize what a dreadful time they are going to have coping with the sorts of contentions raised there, what then? Could it be that *Warth* may stimulate experimentation with mediation approaches precisely because adversary encounters before the courts are increasingly unsuited and unable to reconcile the many positions in multifaceted litigation?

For mediation to succeed, some equalization of resources among various rival interests will be necessary. Particularly at the state and local level, there is still a gross disparity in resources available to some of the interests in critical land use conflicts. Headlines to the contrary, even in Washington, the public interest bar involved in consumer and environmental litigation still numbers fewer than two hundred full-time professionals.

There are other options worth pursuing as well. Perhaps from the Dutch, who subsidize community groups and environmental groups, local and national, we may learn something. The Conservation Foundation's International Comparative Land Use Program is studying carefully not only these sorts of subsidies, but also the use of the referendum in planning and development in Germany, and requirements—such as that in the housing code of Atami, Japan—that consent of all neighbors and interested parties be gained before changes in use be approved. If nothing more, such studies suggest the breadth of nonadversary alternatives for accommodating interests and allocating public benefits and harms, and the room for experimentation in devising such process solutions for Americans. A major issue confronting land use policymakers in the years just ahead will be to choose among such solutions, and to subject them to tests of experience. This way lies the alternative to stalemate, and to the unsatisfying process of repeated resort to protracted litigation.

Afterword

Do all these confusing trends and conflicts seem discouraging? Quite to the contrary, we expect them to provoke new and continuing thought. Environmentalists must no longer think in terms of absolutes, of constraints as imposing stone walls. Rather, constraints are complex phenomena, worthy of more thought and study.

Quality, happily, is becoming a common goal. Does bureaucracy invariably fix upon quantity at the expense of quality? Well, there are some things bureaucracies can do, and there are other things citizens and neighbors can do better.

What we are going to see, we suspect, is a shaking out, a clarifiation of those boundaries. It will be accompanied by lots of discussion, and that may well be as intellectually satisfying, and a whole lot more fun, than the hostility and adrenal confrontation engendered in adversary process.

There are enlarged opportunities for thought and growth and change encompassed in the unfolding new mood. To paraphrase a song from the recent movie "Nashville," for a two-hundred-year-old nation, that isn't half bad.

Notes

1. William K. Reilly (ed.), *The Use of Land: A Citizens' Policy Guide to Urban Growth* (New York: Thos. Y. Crowell Co., September 1973).

2. In fact such an analysis has been written by Phyllis Myers, "Land Policies and Energy Conservation," and appears as Part III in the Energy Conservation Training Manual, published by The Conservation Foundation, 1976.

3. *Use of Land*, p. 17.

4. *Use of Land*, p. 17.

5. *Columbia Journalism Review*, September/October 1975, p. 62.

6. William Watts, and Lloyd A. Free, *State of the Nation 1974* (Potomoc Associates/Harper, 1974).

7. Opinion Research Corporation, "Public Attitudes Toward Environmental Tradeoffs" (Princeton, N.J.: Opinion Research Corporation, August 1975).

8. *Use of Land*, p. 107.

9. *Use of Land*, p. 123.

10. *Use of Land*, p. 143.

11. *Use of Land*, pp. 23-24.

12. *Use of Land*, p. 123.

13. *Use of Land*, pp. 177-178.

14. *Use of Land*, p. 25.

15. *Use of Land*, p. 26.

16. *Use of Land*, pp. 26-27.

17. *Use of Land*, p. 27.

18. Ibid.

19. *Use of Land*, p. 6.

20. *Use of Land*, p. 25.

21. *Use of Land*, p. 28.

22. *Use of Land*, p. 29.

23. Colin Ward speech at "Continuing Heritage" Conference of the Civic Trust of Great Britain and the Royal Institute of British Architects, London, July 1975.

24.

25. *Use of Land*, p. 19.

26. *Use of Land*, p. 239.

27. Sir Keith Joseph speech at "Continuing Heritage" Conference of the Civic Trust of Great Britain and the Royal Institute of British Architects, London, July 1975.

28. Ibid.

Index

Index

About the Authors

ROBERT CAHN is writer-in-residence at The Conservation Foundation and was formerly environment editor of *The Christian Science Monitor.* He currently serves, by presidential appointment, on the fifteen-member Citizens' Advisory Committee on Environmental Quality, and was one of the three original members of the President's Council on Environmental Quality. Mr. Cahn has had a long career as a newspaper and magazine writer and editor. In 1969, he won the Pulitzer Prize for national reporting for a sixteen-part Monitor series: "Will Success Spoil the National Parks."

MICHAEL S. TEITELBAUM is Fellow of Nuffield College and University Lecturer in Demography at Oxford University. He is a former Rhodes Scholar and has served on the professional staff of the Ford Foundation and on the faculty of Princeton University. The author of numerous articles, including "Population and Development: Is a Consensus Possible?" and "Relevance of Demographic Transition Theory for Developing Countries," Dr. Teitelbaum is currently working on a book on the historical demography of nineteenth century England, Wales, Scotland and Ireland.

HARRISON BROWN is professor of geochemistry and science and government at California Institute of Technology. He is a trustee of Resources for the Future, Inc. and the Charles F. Kettering Foundation and is president of the International Council of Scientific Unions. A prolific author, Dr. Brown has contributed many books and articles on population, geochronology, physics and chemistry of the solar system, and science and public policy.

JAMES L. DRAPER is associate director of Central Coast Counties Development Corporation, a nonprofit organization engaged in agriculture-based rural community development in California. His background includes publishing a farm newspaper in Memphis, Tennessee, and heading the rural economic development branch of the Office of Economic Opportunity in Washington.

JON R. ELAM is a "circuit-riding" city administrator for five small communities in southwestern Minnesota. He is a former assistant dean at the University of California at Davis and project director of a National Rural Development Demonstration Project. A former Vista volunteer, Mr. Elam has served as a consultant in a wide range of rural and agricultural development issues over the past ten years.

STEWART BLEDSOE is owner and manager of the Flying B Cattle Ranch in Ellensburg, Washington. He has served as director of the Washington State Department of Agriculture and is president of the Western Association of State Departments of Agriculture. In 1964, he was elected to the Washington State Legislature and served terms as both Majority Whip and Majority Leader. He was a delegate to the People-to-People Tour of the USSR in 1964.

HENRY L. DIAMOND is a partner in the law firm of Ruckelshaus, Beveridge, Fairbanks and Diamond. From December 1973 until March 1974, he served as executive director of the Commission on Critical Choices for Americans. He is chairman of the President's Citizens' Advisory Committee on Environmental Quality. In 1970, Mr. Diamond became New York State's first commissioner of environmental conservation, when a new department was created by the Legislature, combining all state resource management and antipollution programs into the nation's first overall environmental department.

WILLIAM K. REILLY is president of The Conservation Foundation. He was executive director of the Task Force on Land Use and Urban Growth, organized by the Citizens' Advisory Committee on Environmental Quality, and editor of the task force's final report, *The Use of Land: A Citizens' Policy Guide to Urban Growth*. He is a former senior staff member of the President's Council on Environmental Quality and associate director of the Urban Policy Center of Urban America, Inc. (since merged into what is now the National Urban Coalition). He is the author of numerous articles on urban development, land use, public lands, transportation, and environmental impact assessment.

ABOUT THE AUTHORS

JOHN H. NOBLE is advisor to the president of The Conservation Foundation. He was a senior staff member of the Task Force on Land Use and Urban Growth. He is a former assistant director of the American Society of Planning Officials and of the National Commission on Urban Problems. For nearly a decade, he has served as advisor to planning and environmental agencies of the Commonwealth of Puerto Rico.